T0209306

Woodcraft Camps of
DANIEL CARTER BEARD
1912–1938
America's Most Popular Boy Scout

William V. Kahler, Ph.D

WOODCRAFT CAMPS OF DANIEL CARTER BEARD
1912-1938 AMERICA'S MOST POPULAR BOY SCOUT

iUniverse books may be ordered through booksellers or by contacting:

iUniverse
1663 Liberty Drive
Bloomington, IN 47403
www.iuniverse.com
844-349-9409

ISBN: 978-1-6632-2640-2 (sc)
ISBN: 978-1-6632-2639-6 (e)

Library of Congress Control Number: 2021919661

Print information available on the last page.

iUniverse rev. date: 09/28/2021

This book is dedicated to my
three Cub Scout grandsons:

ANDREW AND TYLER YONAVICK

AND

MASON KAHLER

Table of Contents

Part One: Culver Military Academy and the Culver Summer School of Woodcraft

Part Two: The Outdoor School for Boys

ACKNOWLEDGEMENTS

Dan Beard:
America's Most Popular
Boy Scout, 1910-1941

Beard in white buckskin shirt and gloves.
Courtesy of Bear Mountain State Museum.

Assistance is helpful in the creation of most books, and I would like to thank several people, libraries, museums and archives who made this publication possible. Jeff Kenney, Don Fox, and Vicki Pare' Crossley from The Culver Educational Academy for their assistance in providing pictures, newspaper articles and approving part one of the book entitled "Culver Summer School of Woodcraft, 1912 – 1915".

Daniel Bartlett Beard and Barbara Beard Harper, son and daughter of Daniel Carter Beard, who provided me with personal sources, interviews and letter correspondence. In addition, they were helpful in clarifying a number of obscure issues.

Millersville University and Texas A&M library faculty and staff for their thoughtful assistance in securing pertinent data.

Denise Steuhl, Lackawaxen Township Administrative Assistant for her Xeroxing of pictures and articles from the 1998 edition of the Lackawaxen Township Bicentennial Book.

Mathew Shook and Edward McGowan, Bear Mountain State Park Museum, for their assistance in photographing pictures, letters and articles pertaining to Dan Beard.

Dover Publications, for permission to use Beard's illustrations from the reprint of his book: <u>Camp Lore and Woodcraft</u>. Mark Barbernitz, Northeast Council of the Boy Scouts of America, for permission to use pictures and write-up of the Dan Beard cabin project.

David Scott, author of <u>The Scouting Party</u>, for assisting me with the introduction (commonly called "the Hook").

Special thanks to Tara Tappert for editing part one and to Rochelle W. Karapatakis for editing part two and Janis Albuquerque and Mara Stork for their graphic design expertise.

Gratitude is extended to the numerous persons whom the author interviewed for facts and judgments. Also, to those who devoted their time to replying to the lengthy letter requests.

Daniel Carter Wing, for information from a camp scrapbook provided to him by his Grandmother, Alice Beard Finney.

FOREWORD

DANIEL CARTER BEARD:
OUTDOORSMAN and LEADER of AMERICAN YOUTH

Seldom does a man become a legendary hero of American boyhood during his lifetime. However, still standing out as the most popular Boy Scout leader in American history, Daniel Carter Beard had the extraordinary privilege of being the living inspiration of tens-of-thousands of boys in the United States of America and even the entire world from 1910 – 1941. Answering questions from readers of his outdoor articles in Scouting's <u>Boys' Life</u> magazine was the personal touch that caused the young boys to give him the alias "Uncle Dan." Uncle Dan, by word and by deed, established himself as considerably worthy of hero-worship. A small, spry, Vandyke-bearded man with white hair and a wrinkled face, dressed for ceremonial occasions in buckskin, awed boys with frontier-yarns and with an actual Bald Eagle's claw dubbed Eagle Scouts. Uncle Dan's commitment to the Boy Scouts of America and to the well-being of adolescent boys is reflected in a comment his son Bartlett often heard his father say to friends and family: "I WOULD RATHER BE A BOY SCOUT THAN A DICTATOR, KING, OR EVEN PRESIDENT OF THE U.S.A." Daniel Carter Beard was a beloved leader of American youth whose career with the Boy Scouts integrated values such as trustworthiness, responsible citizenship, and self-reliance with participation in outdoor activities such as camping, hiking, and crafting. The wholesome standards and goals initiated by Beard more than one hundred years ago still continue to better America's youth today.

Thousands knew Beard personally, but only a few knew of the

many portions of his amazing long career. Beard lived 91 years, born less than 75 years after the Declaration of Independence was signed and entered into rest in 1941. His birthplace was Cincinnati, Ohio, on June 21, 1850. In those days, a man who journeyed alone into the wilderness beyond the Ohio River either lived or died by his own survival abilities. Most of Beard's youth was spent in the enthusiastic cult of the out-of-doors and woodcraft. In 1861 the Beard family moved from Cincinnati, Ohio, across the Ohio River to Covington, Kentucky. Beard took great pleasure in his new rural surroundings of forests and rivers. He made friends easily and with his gang of friends roamed the woods where they pretended to be pioneers in the spirit of Daniel Boone, the frontiersman who spearheaded Kentucky's settlement a century earlier. He enjoyed the games, outdoor pursuits and river adventures so common to boys his age. Later in life he would relate stories concerning his gang of "Boone Scouts." It seemed like everybody in the Covington and Newport, Kentucky, area knew of the diverse sizes and shapes of Beard's kites that he learned to build. He made kites shaped like men, women, children, birds, butterflies and fish. It was his giant eight-feet long kites that drew public attention. During his boyhood, his learning of woodcraft, handicraft and Indian lore strengthened his love of the outdoors. Indeed, one might also imagine that Mark Twain had taken Beard as the prototype of his Tom Sawyer, if we did not know that he himself had enjoyed a similar childhood in the broad free West. He learned the Star-Spangled Brand of Americanism and Patriotism by the influence of his pioneering parents and preached and inculcated it to millions of Americans throughout his lifetime.

Another characteristic of Beard was an interest in the arts. He was practically born in an art studio. His father, James H. Beard painted portraits and group scenes, and bestowed to his children an intrinsic desire to create art. (He urged his children not to follow his profession, however, because of the insecurity of the career.) Dan's inclination to sketch, in addition to his outdoor adventures along the Ohio and Licking Rivers and the forests surrounding Covington, led him to use his skill in sketching wildlife. As a young adult, he chose to train as an engineer and surveyor rather than an artist. Beard had attended the public school system in Covington, Kentucky. He furthered his education at Worrall's Academy in Covington, majoring in Civil Engineering. He graduated with honors in 1869, worked for the City Engineer of Cincinnati, Ohio, and in 1874 joined the Sanborn Map and Company. He traveled throughout the United States, preparing maps for insurance companies. Loneliness, occupational frustration, and family urging finally persuaded him to abandon surveying in favor of illustrating, and so in 1887, he joined his family in New York City. That was the beginning of what Beard termed "a self-styled sixty-three-year vacation." Thanks in part to a gadgetry forte, Beard proved successful in the writing and illustrating industry. During the late 1880's he served as an illustrator for Mark Twain and wrote and illustrated the most widely read and recognized books and magazine articles regarding the outdoors. His most popular book, The American Boys Handy Book: What To Do And How To Do It (1882), sold an estimated 250,000 copies and became the standard of American Juvenile Literature. The book was a do-it-yourself guide to outdoor fun and woodcraft and handicraft skills that was organized into seasonal activities for the readers. His zest for turning endless play into "play with a purpose" was responsible for landing him in the early stages of the youth service movement. Through his magazine articles and boys writing to him for advice on outdoor topics, a national boy's movement was established called "Sons of Daniel Boone." Later renamed "Boy

Pioneers," both programs had a clear focus on the American frontier, but the movement had no national administrative organization. The boys learned the program by reading Beard's articles/ideas in various children's magazines. A constitution was developed and the objective clearly stated: "…to teach the boys how to form clubs for the purpose of enjoying outdoor fun in a healthy, wholesome, boyish manner; also, for the purpose of preserving American traditions, plants and animals, of encouraging American boys to emulate all that was best in the lives of their pioneer ancestors, and advocating and supporting the laws prohibiting the sale of game." By 1910, when Beard chose to merge his magazine youth group into the American Boy Scout Movement, it was estimated that approximately 20,000 boys merged into the Scouting Movement. This merger ultimately set the table for his 30-plus years as National Scout Commissioner, president of the Camp Fire Club of America, president of the Society of Illustrators, editor of the boys' department of Pictorial Review, and illustrator of outdoor books among a multitude of other roles.

For almost three decades, Beard had a direct association with young boys through his involvement with outdoor summer woodcraft camps. His first involvement was with the Culver Military Academy Woodcraft Camp from 1912 – 1915. From 1916 – 1938 he structured the Dan Beard Outdoor School for Boys, later changed to the Dan Beard Camp, Inc., on Lake Teedyuskung, near Hawley, Pennsylvania. This is a book about these early camps founded on sound principles by Daniel Carter Beard, America's most famous Boy Scout leader from 1910 -1941 who knew woodcraft, and the adventurous spirit of boys, and loved them both.

INTRODUCTION

I n early January, 1917, a letter arrived at the home office of Daniel Carter Beard. Dated December 29, 1916, it read—

I was glad to get your letter and I hope that I can come to your camp next year, and bring my friend Dudley Sharpes. I have joined the YMCA and like it very much. Enclosed please find my Buckskin Badge. I have returned it on account of eating some candy.

With love from Howard

P.S. I hope that you and Mrs. Beard and Bartlett and Barbara have a happy New Year.

The letter, from a shy and timid ten-year-old from Houston, Texas, references the Outdoor School for Boys, a camp opened on a lake in Pennsylvania during the summer of 1916 by the extraordinary outdoorsman and youth leader Dan Beard. His camp was just one of the many ways in the early decades of the twentieth century that Beard encouraged and promoted the lives of American boys.

In 1916 the Beard family was living in Flushing, New York. Their children, Barbara and Bartlett, attended private schools, and Dan maintained a busy home office, from which he created book and magazine illustrations, wrote articles, and served as Associate Editor of *Boys' Life*, the official magazine of the Boy Scouts of America. Beard was also a naturalist, a woodsman, and a camp director, and from his books about the outdoors and his articles in *Boys' Life*, a reader could imagine the broad western prairies and the unexplored trails in the mountains and rivers. Dan Beard, who was one of the founders of the Boy Scouts of America, was "Uncle Dan" to millions of boys and their fathers, was regarded as a real frontiersman, the last of America's pioneers, he was the symbol of scouting, and the "Spiritual Father" of this largest youth organization in the world.

In 1911, with headquarters in New York City, the Boy Scouts of America quickly grew under the able leadership of Chief Scout Executive, Dr. James West. The Scouts purchased *Boys' Life* in 1912, and Dan Beard's monthly columns of personal anecdotes, handicraft and woodcraft instruction, and lessons on patriotism were eagerly read.

Incorporated in 1910, the Boy Scouts of America was awarded a national charter on June 15, 1916 that granted them sole claim to the name "Boy Scouts."

Another law passed by Congress shortly thereafter barred competing youth groups from wearing the official Boy Scout uniform, which Dan Beard helped design. A Boy Scout in his official uniform is easily recognized.

His articles were so popular that West provided Beard with a new desk and typewriter for his home office, as well as secretarial assistance. West understood Beard had achieved an iconic standing within the scouting world.

From his service as a National Scout Commissioner and his role as the Associate Editor of *Boys' Life*, Beard became an American folk hero. No other scout official was so broadly identified with American youth. As a picturesque character who looked and dressed like a wilderness scout in a white buckskin uniform, and who told colorful stories of early pioneer life, Dan Beard was the American scout personified. He served on the Executive Board and National Council, participating in committees responsible for developing scouting policies and programs. He was thrust into a mentoring role for both local and national scout volunteers when he was appointed National Scout Commissioner. As chairperson of the National Court of Honor he presided over deliberations of rewards for scouts recognized for heroic or meritorious acts of service. He was the only member of the National Council whose life was primarily devoted to Boy Scout activities. For more than three decades Dan Beard guided the organization and captivated the boys who participated as scouts.

From 1912 to 1938, Dan Beard's most direct association with adolescent boys was through camps for ten to eighteen-year-olds. He first led a woodcraft summer school from 1912 to 1915 at the Culver Military Academy in Culver, Indiana. While he was a law unto himself at Culver, he chafed under some real limitations. Influencing his decision to open his own boys' camp were the unsatisfactory living conditions endured by his family, the humid climate, and the camp's military atmosphere. In 1916 Beard opened the Outdoor School for Boys at his property on Lake Teedyuskung in Hawley, Pennsylvania. There he provided comfortable living facilities, good food, and instruction in outdoor living and nature. Known as "Chief," Beard was the camp's major attraction. Dressed in his buckskin pants, shirt, and moccasins, he told stories of patriotic events and pioneers, encouraged his campers to enjoy the outdoors, and helped them develop woodcraft skills. The boys responded with affection, awe, respect, and devotion.

The ten-year-old who had written Beard during the Christmas holidays of 1916 attended the Outdoor School for Boys the first year the camp was open. Beard's young correspondent was Howard "Sonny" R. Hughes, Jr. Friends had suggested to Sonny's over-protective and strict mother, Allene Hughes, that "it was time to make a man out of Howard." The boy idolized his mother, but her friends thought he was "sissified" and a "mommy's boy."

Howard was undoubtedly regarded as one of those children who could benefit from a summer camp experience that offered discipline and rugged training. Many affluent families during the first decades of the twentieth century sent their children to summer camps while they vacationed in Europe. Allene Hughes entrusted her son to Dan Beard, with the hope that he would learn to interact with other young boys, and that an outdoors experience would enhance what she considered his "fragile constitution."

Howard Hughes (1905-1976) was an American business tycoon, investor, aviator, aerospace engineer, inventor, filmmaker, and philanthropist. During his lifetime he was known as the "wealthiest, self-made man in the world."

His father was the successful inventor, businessman, and wildcatter, Howard Robard Hughes, Sr., who founded the Hughes Tool Company; and his mother, Allene Gano, was a Dallas, Texas heiress who was a descendant of John Gano, the minister known to have baptized George Washington. Howard's best friends when he was a child, were his young neighbors, Dudley and Mary Sharpe.

Mrs. Hughes wrote to Beard on June 14, 1916—

My Dear Mr. Beard:

I have received your catalogue and letter of May 29th and we have heard much of your camp from Mr. Thompson and his boys [who had attended the Culver Woodcraft School]. *Mr. Hughes and I feel that the life at your camp and your personal influence will be of great benefit to Howard and* [we] *are enclosing his application for entrance this summer. There are a few questions we want to ask and will very much appreciate your answering by wire. Do you take boys as young as Howard?*

How many boys his age will you probably have in camp?

What will your total enrollment be?

This will be Howard's first experience away from his family and we think it desirable to place him in a rather small camp for this first year at least.

Beard assured the concerned mother that his wife would personally look after her son, and that his own nine-year-old son, Bartlett, would also be at camp along with other boys Howard's age.

Howard's camping experience during the summer of 1916 was just what his mother wanted. He became a Boy Scout, earned his tenderfoot and second class ranks, and excelled in merit badge requirements for aviation, first aid, camping, cooking and swimming. Yet his greatest honor that summer was selection by the camp instructors to become one of the "Buckskin Men." He had demonstrated the required standards of character and integrity, and was initiated into this novel fraternity by closing his eyes, placing his right hand on Beard's supposed "Indian scalp," and reciting a pledge, oath, and promise. Each of the honored boys then wore a buckskin badge branded with the powder horn of Daniel Boone. It was the camp's most highly prized award.

A review of the childhood camp accomplishments of the later notorious, widely publicized, and mysterious Howard Hughes, come from evaluations by his instructors—

> He cannot stick to one thing very long, but is doing fairly well in scoutcraft and never gives us any trouble. In birds, his effort and deportment is good. In his other studies he is trying hard, but is easily discouraged. Needs someone to show him how and then make him do it.

And from Beard, who noted—

> He did very good work in scoutcraft. In the beginning he didn't care so much, but he soon got to be a hard little worker and passed his Tenderfoot and Second Class Scout degrees.

The joyful and admiring relationship between Beard and his campers was captured in the repentant letter of the adolescent Hughes who willingly returned his buckskin badge because he had eaten a piece of candy. As a teenager during the 1920s Hughes visited the camp several summers, and in his later life proudly recalled his association with Dan Beard.

The Chief's commitment to the Boy Scouts of America and to the well-being of adolescent boys is reflected in a comment his son Bartlett often heard his father say to friends and family—

"I WOULD RATHER BE A BOY SCOUT THAN A DICTATOR, KING, OR EVEN PRESIDENT OF THE USA."

Daniel Carter Beard was a beloved leader of American youth whose career with the Boy Scouts encompassed positive promotion of character values—trustworthiness, responsible citizenship, self-reliance—and participation in outdoor activities—camping, hiking, crafting. These wholesome standards and healthful accomplishments initiated by Beard more than one hundred years ago for the betterment of America's youth continue to this day.

Photo of Dan Beard from the cover of *Boys' Life* magazine, May, 1914, Headline announcing "Mr. Dan Beard and Mr. Ernest Thompson Seton Become the Associate Editors" of the magazine.

PART ONE

CULVER MILITARY ACADEMY

AND THE

CULVER SUMMER SCHOOL OF WOODCRAFT

Under the Direction of Dan Beard
1912-1915

"Culver Academy ... possesses the distinction of being the first academic institution to add woodcraft to its course of studies, and is modeled on the Boy Scouts."

—Daniel Carter Beard (1912)

THE ACADEMY AND ITS
FIRST SUMMER SCHOOLS

The Culver Military Academy was founded in 1894 on the shores of Lake Maxinkuckee in northern Indiana. From its beginnings, the Academy's founder, a St. Louis businessman named Henry Harrison Culver, envisioned an institution managed within a military framework. It was noted in the Academy's first catalog that such an approach would offer *a particular advantage in bringing about the best results in the development of boys.*

H. H. Culver met his wife, Emily Jane Hand, in the 1860s, while he was on a business trip that brought him to the northeast corner of Lake Maxinkuckee, where she was a school teacher. The couple moved to the lake for health reasons in 1883, and built a home. By the following year Culver had purchased, for development, 300 acres of lakefront and surrounding property. His first business venture was a supporting hotel for the Culver Park Assembly, one

Lake Maxinkuckee is a large natural lake in the state of Indiana. It covers 1,864 acres and is located near the town of Culver. Its name, "Maxinkuckee," is derived from the Potawatomi Indian word "mog-sin-ke-ki" which means "Big Stone Country."

of the Chautauqua revival programs known for attracting tens of thousands of visitors. But the Assembly failed to flourish, and Culver, who had opened the hotel in 1889, was forced, for financial reasons, to close it just two years later.

While starting a school had been one of Culver's *castles in the air*, by the 1890s his daydream had become a reality. He noted that he *saw in* [his] *mind's eye where the school would have to be.* By 1894 Culver had converted his hotel into dormitories, class-rooms, and support facilities, and that year—Culver Military Institute—opened its doors to forty-seven boys. The following year, in honor of the community's entrepreneurial businessman and school's founder, the town changed its name from Marmont to Culver. Less than twenty years later, the Culver Military Academy was described in its 1912 promotional catalog as *the most complete and up-to-date school plant in the country.*

In 1902 the Academy opened the Naval School; it was their first summer school program. Its popularity led to the opening in 1907 of the Cavalry School. Together, these eight-week summer programs were so successful that by 1914 they had acquired an international reputation, and 465 boys, aged fourteen and older, arrived from every state in the Union.

For several years parents of boys in the Naval and Cavalry schools asked the Culver trustees if they would bend the age requirement so their younger sons could attend. Rather than risk the safety of boys not yet ready for such strenuous naval and cavalry training, a decision was made to open a woodcraft school

CULVER MILITARY ACADEMY

is situated on Lake Maxenkuckee, Indiana, in a beautiful park of 80 acres, containing campus, fine course for cavalry practice, track for bicycle and sprinting races, lawn tennis and base ball grounds, gymnasium, (70x80 feet), six flowing artesian wells, etc. The lake is one of the most beautiful in the United States, covers an area of about 12 square miles, is wholly fed by springs, has a beautiful gently sloping beach, and is a most pleasant and popular summer resort, affording opportunity for all kinds of aquatic sports. The Academy and Dormitory building is complete in every particular, entirely new ABSOLUTELY FIRE PROOF, finished in hard wood, heated by steam lighted by electricity, has hot and cold water baths, lavatories, and all toilet conveniences. The course of study prepares cadets for college, scientific schools, business, West Point or Annapolis. The Academy is under the supervision of a West Point graduate and ex-army officer of large experience in teaching, who will have direct control of the discipline of the cadets.
For further information and catalogue address:
Culver Military Academy, Marmont, Ind.

Culver Military Academy newspaper ad, from the *Culver Herald*, circa 1896.

that could accommodate those under the age of fourteen. In 1912, the Culver Summer School of Woodcraft opened and quickly achieved high regard. Its success came from the military academy's financial commitment to its summer programs, the popularity of the emergent Scouting Movement, and Culver's ability to attract leaders with well-recognized experience working with and inspiring boys.

Lieutenant Colonel Leigh R. Gignilliat, Superintendent of the Culver Military Academy, was interested in the growing Boy

Scout Movement, begun in England in 1907 under the leadership of Sir Robert Baden-Powell. Superintendent Gignilliat made a trip to England to meet the man, and was so impressed with the idea of scouting that he invited Sir Baden-Powell to visit the Academy on his next journey to America. Boy Scout business brought Sir Baden-Powell to the U.S. in 1912, and because of his own military background, he included a stopover at Culver.

Sir Robert Baden-Powell was a British Army officer, writer, and the author of "Scouting for Boys." This publication was an inspiration in the founding of the Boy Scout Movement in England, in 1907. Baden-Powell was the first Chief Scout of The Boy Scouts Association, and was also the founder of the Girl Guides. His work in England laid the foundation for scouting in America, with Boy Scout programs beginning in the U.S. in 1910.

During his visit to Culver, Sir Baden-Powell and Superintendent Gignilliat traversed the Academy's expansive acreage of athletic fields, broad green lawns, and forest lands. As they walked they discussed the kinds of training and educational programs that would be enjoyable and of interest and benefit to younger boys. Following an inspection of the grounds and the Academy facilities, Sir Baden-Powell stated—

> I have seen the cadets of all nationalities at their work, but I must say you beat the lot. Your organization and superb equipment are a revelation to me.

The beautiful lakefront property and wooded acres surrounding the Academy offered unique opportunities for a myriad of outdoor pursuits—aquatic activities, as well as the study of trees, flowers, birds, and fish. By the end of Sir Baden-Powell's visit,

Superintendent Gignilliat had committed to developing a summer camp for younger boys that would focus on woodcraft and nature activities.

The question then arose as to whom they should approach to help establish and direct the Culver Summer School of Woodcraft. Neither Superintendent Gignilliat nor Sir Baden-Powell was able to take on the task. Gignilliat was a trained military man but not a naturalist, and Sir Baden-Powell had his hands full managing the growing world-wide Scouting Movement. In considering possible candidates they decided the best person to lead the school was Daniel Carter Beard. He was well-known and highly respected throughout the country, and his qualifications were further confirmed when Superintendent Gignilliat attended a lecture by prominent conservationist and forester, Gifford Pinchot, who was also the 28th Governor of Pennsylvania. Pinchot noted—

> *Mr. Beard has taught the boys of two generations more woodcraft than any man in America. Certainly this great boys' man has a knack of making things more interesting and the eight weeks seem all too short to the boys under his instruction.*

Dan Beard was a nationally recognized youth leader. He was also the director of a successful service organization—Sons of Daniel Boone, renamed Boy Pioneers of America—that was later merged with the Boy Scouts of America. He was a leader in the emerging Boy Scouts Movement, serving as the National Scout Commissioner of the Boy Scouts of America, and was also the President of The Camp Fire Club of America. In his professional life, Beard was president of the Society of Illustrators, and editor of the "Boys' Department" of *Pictorial Review*. Boys and young men enjoyed reading Beard's books, and enthusiastically completed activities he laid out for them in *The American Boys' Handy Book* and in *Jack of All Trades*. Beard's youth service organization was promoted in articles written for *Women's Home Companion* and *Pictorial Review*, and millions of boys eagerly anticipated his monthly columns. As far as Superintendent Gignilliat and Sir Baden-Powell were concerned, Dan Beard had the organizational and leadership skills needed to successfully develop a woodcraft summer school at Culver.

In March 1912, Superintendent Gignilliat placed a phone call to Dan Beard, and after much persuasion the hard-working author and illustrator agreed to accept the appointment of "Officer in Immediate Charge." In addition to his monthly magazine columns and service organization work, Beard had contracts with *Outing*, and *Field and Stream*, and was in the process of writing several books. Nevertheless, that spring, when the Culver Military Academy issued its first catalog for the Summer School of Woodcraft, its subtitle read "Under Direction of Dan Beard," and most of the sketches illustrating the catalog were created by Beard at his own drawing board.

The powerful alliance between the nationally recognized naturalist and woodsman and the mid-western military academy is well-captured by the cover illustration of the summer school's first advertising brochure, sent out in the spring of 1912. A silhouette of four boys gathered around a woodland campfire cooking their supper, not only represented the abundant forest land resources of the Academy, but also skills the boys would be taught by America's best known Boy Scout leader. That first summer proved Culver's

Summer School of Woodcraft was going to be an educational and financial success.

First catalog of the Culver School of Woodcraft, 1912, Courtesy of the Culver Academies Archives, Culver, Indiana.

Daniel Carter Beard with two Woodcraft Campers, 1913. Courtesy of the Culver Academies Archives, Culver, Indiana.

THE CULVER SUMMER SCHOOL OF WOODCRAFT

T hroughout the spring and early summer of 1912 Dan Beard conveyed a wealth of knowledge to those planning the new Culver Summer School of Woodcraft. From his work between 1905 and 1910 creating and administering the Sons of Daniel Boone and Boy Pioneers of America, he had gained an understanding of the interests of American youth and a sound awareness of their physical capabilities. The visioning process for the new school not only reflected Beard's club and outdoor experiences, but also Superintendent Gignilliat's keen interest in the Boy Scout Movement, and the understanding of Culver staff members regarding the value of military procedure. Together, with Beard, Culver faculty designed a summer program that blended the school's approach to discipline and organization with the naturalist's educational and recreational expertise. Beard's famous maxim—*A boy, like a tree, grows best with his toes in the ground*—

offered a foundational principle for the new school and for the training of young boys.

> Woodcraft developed from early outdoor camping. It is "the knowledge of how to properly perform when in the woods." Woodcraft skills include: preparing for a camping trip; choosing a campsite; preparing a shelter and bedding; cooking; the use of a knife, axe, and saw; and the making of many kinds of campfires, such as a Council Fire, for which there are specific rituals. Woodcraft and handicraft skills give campers the training needed to survive in the outdoors.

For the first year of the program, in order to personally interact with each camper and to promote meaningful relationships with their instructors, the Culver administration set enrollment at forty boys, aged twelve and thirteen. Culver regarded the initial year as an experiment, with technique and safety as the overriding purpose rather than income. Only thirty-six attended in 1912, but the numbers steadily increased during the four years Dan Beard was the director—fifty-eight in 1913, eighty-three in 1914, and 140 in 1915. Culver also maintained its commitment to hands-on involvement with the campers, and for every ten boys in attendance, school staff was increased accordingly.

As plans solidified in 1912 for the opening of the woodcrafters' school, Culver staff sent a message to parents that clearly communicated an experience at the new camp would be an invigorating summer adventure—

> *There is a period in every boy's development corresponding perhaps to a similar stage in the evolution of the race, during which he is peculiarly susceptible to the influence of the open. A period in which nature herself may become his teacher, imparting to him lessons of resourcefulness, courage and patience, and planting in him a love for the open, such that he may return to it after years for refreshment*

In the center is Mr. Beard and sitting on the ground Bartlett Beard, the Camp Mascot.

Top Row: Bale, H. S., Ohio; Litchfield, S. G., New York; Babb, J. T., Idaho; Palmer, G. D., Indiana; Marmon, H., Indiana; Lammert, W. B., Missouri; Powell, W. B., Illinois; Hopson, R. N., Mississippi; Perkins, W. H., Maryland; Engle, A. J., Kansas; Gates, E. E., Indiana.
Second Row: Tisch, R. W., Michigan; Fawcett, J. E., Ohio; Hood, K., Jr., Kentucky; Henson, G. W., Illinois; Munn, L., Texas; Parker, J. L., Ohio; Love, G. H., Pennsylvania; Van Nes, H. C., Ohio; Tryon, J. A., Texas; Browning, S. P., Jr., Kentucky.
Third Row: Hood, H., Kentucky; Holder, D. S., Louisiana; Dobbs, R. H., Kansas; Wetmore, H. O., Illinois; Broyles, N. A., Georgia; Fitch, G. W., Iowa; Googins, J. C., Texas; Rounds, J. M., Illinois; Brown, E. A., Jr., Georgia; Caswell, J. H., Indiana; Allen, D. B., Ohio; Robertson, J. J., Missouri; Clark C. W., Mississippi.
Fourth Row: Smith, L. M., Missouri; Logan, W. M., Texas; Buckner, C. M., Jr., Missouri; Barnaby, H. P., Indiana; Stilwell, N. C., Indiana; Jacobs, L. G., Michigan; Sanford, L. A., Ohio; Wyatt, W. W., Ohio; Mattox, R. C., Indiana; Hill, R. C., Ohio; Flowers, J. P., Illinois; Morley, D. M., Washington.
Fifth Row: Kindig, J. K., Pennsylvania; Engle, E. T., Kansas; Brady, F.A., Illinois; Lammert. M. O., Missouri; Lt. James H. Beard; Jackson, S. D. L., Jr., Ohio; Mr. Dan Beard; McLallen, D. L., Indiana; Logue E. A., Pennsylvania; Grover, E. H. Indiana; McFarland, J., Iowa; Long, P., Ohio.

The 1913 Summer School of Woodcraft; fifty-eight boys attended. They hailed from Idaho, Indiana, Kansas, Kentucky, Maryland, Mississippi, Missouri, New York, Ohio, Pennsylvania, and Texas. Courtesy of the Culver Academies Archives, Culver, Indiana.

and inspiration. It is to boys at this stage that Culver offers the summer course in Woodcraft. This outing will be a rare privilege for any boy and whether he has camped or tramped the woods or not, the association with Mr. Beard will be an inspiration, as well as an experience full of interest and practical value.

In the months leading up to the opening of the school, *The Culver Citizen* satisfied the curiosity of community members with newspaper articles about the summer program. One from March

21

28, 1912, detailed the purpose of the school and highlighted its association with the Boy Scout Movement—

The most notable feature of the work for 1912 is the new school of Woodcraft for younger boys which will be under the personal supervision of the great master of woodcraft in America, Mr. Dan Beard. The number of boys aged 12 and 13 who have always desired to attend the summer school and some of whom have usually been accepted has been more or less a handicap to the larger boys as the little fellows were not equal to the task of handling either the rifles or the big oars. Consequently, the new department will take care of all the new boys as young as twelve and will give them plenty of interesting and profitable work of exactly the kind that delights a boy's heart and in addition will leave the Navel and Cavalry battalion in better condition to do the required work. The Woodcrafters will be in a camp by themselves east of the present Cavalry Street and provision is being made to take care of forty boys. In the entire country probably no better man could have been secured to take charge of the work than Mr. Dan Beard. He is one of the most frequent contributors on outdoor subjects to magazines, he edits such an outdoor magazine himself, is the author of numerous books over which thousands of boys pour [over] by the hour learning the craft of the woodsman and he is one of the joint founders of the American Boy Scouts as Gen. Baden-Powell was of the English movement.

Because the school's woodcraft theme originated from Super-intendent Gignilliat's interest in the newly emerging Boy Scout Movement in America, during its inaugural year Boy Scout troop leaders came to Culver to participate in two weeks of programming.

Culver Summer Schools newspaper ad featuring Dan Beard at the Woodcraft School, as it appeared in *Boys' Life* magazine, circa 1913. Courtesy of the Culver Academies Archives, Culver, Indiana.

The men attended lectures, learned woodcraft and handicraft skills, and assessed the supervision of the camp. Its activities were also closely followed by Chief Scout Executive of the Boy Scouts of America, James E. West. He was interested in the camp and how it might benefit his organization in the future. One of the Scout troop leaders, Allen March—leader of Troop #1 in Plymouth, Indiana—responded to a query from West regarding his experience at Culver during the summer of 1912. March wrote Chief Scout Executive West—

> *I went to Culver on the first of August and remained there until the fifteenth. During which time I studied the Scout Movement and observed the work being done in the Woodcraft Camp under the supervision of Mr. Daniel*

Carter Beard. I cannot speak too highly of the benefits I derived from this fifteen-day course. I came back to Plymouth filled with confidence and enthusiasm and found the work of organizing Plymouth Troop 1 of the Boy Scouts of America comparatively easy and very delightful. I feel that no other school is capable of doing more for the Boy Scout Movement than Culver Military Academy.

Superintendent Gignilliat had developed a woodcraft camp at Culver that reflected the goals and ambitions of the emergent Boy Scout Movement of America, and he had secured Dan Beard, the best-known woodsman in the country, as its leader. It was a most auspicious beginning.

ADMISSION, UNIFORMS, AND EQUIPMENT

 s the Culver Summer School of Woodcraft grew, boys arrived from nearly every section of the country. And early camp catalogs described the advantage of such a geographically diverse enrollment—

Boys come from both Atlantic and Pacific coasts, and each summer in an increasing number from the southern states, parents in the south finding that they cannot do better for their sons then to send them into a more bracing climate for the summer, under the favorable conditions existing at Culver. The broadening influence of this intermingling of boys from widely separated localities is in itself not the least among the advantages offered by the school. Parents who are going abroad or who contemplate other plans necessitating separation from their children during the summer may place them at Culver with the comfortable assurance that they will be well cared for as if they were in their own homes.

Parents were required to complete a comprehensive admissions form. It included personal data, medical information, and a listing of any physical limitations their son might have that would be of importance to the school's instructors. During the eight-week summer terms of 1914 and 1915, tuition was a pricey $150.00, with an additional uniform and equipment fee of $25.00. The boys who attended came from wealthy families, and the fees paid covered tuition, board, uniforms, music, swimming, boxing, and dancing lessons, studies, the use of the library and gymnasium, and other forms of entertainment such as guest lectures and twenty-four pieces of laundry a week.

The Culver uniform was a warm-weather outfit similar to the American Boy Scout uniform. The entire ensemble consisted of one pair of gray cloth shorts, six pairs of stockings with cuffs, two gray flannel shirts with button pockets, one pair of blue serge shorts, one belt, one pair of oiled leather moccasins, two khaki shirts,

An idea of just how expensive it was to attend the Woodcraft camp and purchase uniforms and equipment is suggested by a comparison of 1914 and 1915 costs to their equivalents in 2020. Today, the $150.00 camp tuition equals $3,650.00, while the $25.00 uniform and equipment fee amounts to $608.00.

Dan Beard designed the official Boy Scouts of America uniform in 1911, and it served as the model in 1912 for Culver's summer ensemble for Woodcrafters. Every part of the medium-brown Boy Scout uniform was patterned after clothing worn by American frontiersmen and cowboys, as well as Teddy Roosevelt's Rough Riders.

The broad-brimmed Campaign Hat was based on those worn by frontiersmen. It provided shade and could hold drinking water. The four-pocketed tunic with its button-down high "choker" collar, and the baggy trousers tucked into canvas leggings (known as "puttees") were copied from the U.S. Army uniform of the Rough Riders. The neckerchief was like the cowboy bandana. It could serve as a first aid sling, bandage, and face shield during dust and rain storms.

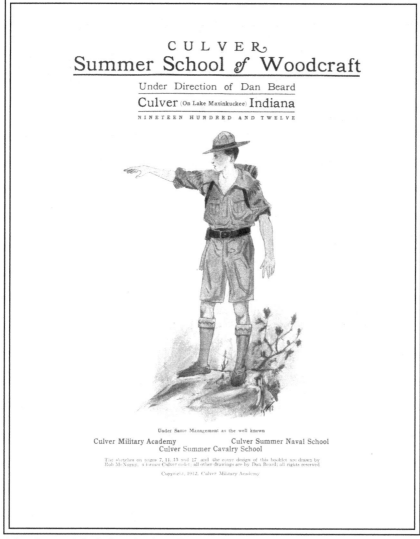

CULVER
Summer School *of* Woodcraft
Under Direction of Dan Beard
Culver (On Lake Maxinkuckee) Indiana
NINETEEN HUNDRED AND TWELVE

Under Same Management as the well known
Culver Military Academy   Culver Summer Naval School
Culver Summer Cavalry School

The sketches on pages 7, 11, 15 and 17, and the cover design of this booklet are drawn by
Rob McNagny, a former Culver cadet; all other drawings are by Dan Beard; all rights reserved.

Copyright, 1912, Culver Military Academy

Culver Summer School of Woodcraft catalog, 1912. Illustration shows the Woodcraft uniform that was designed by Dan Beard, based upon the uniform worn by the Boys Scouts. Courtesy of the Culver Academies Archives, Culver, Indiana.

and two pairs of khaki shorts. The equipment provided included one cooking kit with haversack, a pocket knife (sometimes called a jackknife), and a hatchet (also called an axe) with scabbard.

The various pieces represented different uniforms, and the correct combinations had to be worn for weather and camp activities, and at certain times of the day–at dinner, for example. Some Woodcraft campers who were also Boy Scouts were known to bring their own uniforms to camp and wear them as they earned their merit badges and other Scouting awards.

HOW THE WOODCRAFT
CAMPERS LIVED

The first site for the Woodcrafters School was the once wooded slope in front of the present day Memorial Chapel on the Culver campus, with the headquarters cabin at the road where the base of the chapel steps are now located. Also at the camp site was a pioneer cabin that had been moved there from a hillside near Lake Maxinkuckee, and was later converted into the Indian Lore office and used for small group meetings. Beard suggested that a woodcraft museum be established and also a rainy day meeting cabin, and both were opened by the Culver administration for the 1913 camp year. Two years later, in 1915, the camp was laid out with six streets—Fifth Avenue, Broadway, Main Street, Pennsylvania Avenue, Boulevard, and Wall Street.

Woodcrafters had the use of all the Culver buildings, but the location of their camp on the campus was separated from

The pioneer log cabin was moved to the Woodcraft Camp in 1913, where it became the Woodcraft Museum and rainy day meeting house. The whalebones were placed in front of the cabin a number of years later. Courtesy of the Culver Academies Archives, Culver, Indiana.

Interior of a Woodcrafter's tent—the flaps in the upper panels could be raised or lowered at will from the inside. The tent fly makes the tents rain proof. The raised wooden floors provided for dry and sanitary conditions. The fly, or double roof, extended beyond the front of the tent, allowing for a covered area outside the sleeping bay. Courtesy of the Culver Academies Archives, Culver, Indiana.

the sites of the Naval and Cavalry camps. The older boys were quartered in Culver buildings, but Dan Beard wanted his campers to live as close to nature as possible. He insisted the Woodcrafters live in tents and not in barracks. Their living quarters consisted of twenty tents with two boys per tent, and with instructors similarly housed throughout the camp complex. To ensure dry and sanitary conditions, these fixed tents were weatherproofed against rain and dampness, were on raised floors, and were ventilated by screened openings in the upper half of the side walls, offering protection from insects. Each camper was supplied with a "Gold Medal" cot, a foot locker, and bedding. The tents were arranged in close proximity to promote a sense of "togetherness" and for the boys to sleep as if they were in the open air.

All the summer school campers—Naval, Cavalry, and

One of the noteworthy structures on the Culver campus was the brick and stone Tudor-Gothic style Gymnasium, called the "Little Gym." Built between 1903 and 1904, on the site of the current Reuben H. Fleet Gymnasium, the $50,000, state-of-the-art facility was destroyed by fire in 1906, but using the original architectural plans, it was rebuilt, re-opening in 1907. At the time it was the largest and most complete private school gymnasium in existence. The main gymnasium hall, with polished hard maple floors, had white enamel brick walls, capped by a heavy oak rail, to which were fastened pulley weights and other wall equipment. Opening into the main hall were rooms with designated purposes— an apparatus room, a measuring room, a locker room, a drying room, baths and showers, and a director's room.

The gymnasium itself was well equipped with parallel bars, flying rings, long horses, and buck climbing ladders. There were also climbing ropes, horizontal ladders, felt tumbling and spotting mats, boxing speed bags and spotting belts. There was also a piano.

For the next sixty years, until it was destroyed by fire in 1977, the "Little Gym" was used not only as a gymnasium, but also for lectures, theatrical programs, and religious services.

The "Little Gym" at Culver Military Academy, circa 1911, Courtesy of the Culver Academies Archives, Culver, Indiana.

The dining hall used by all the campers—Naval, Cavalry, and Woodcrafters—through 1916, when a state-of-the-art mess tent was erected for the Woodcraft campers in 1917. Courtesy of the Culver Academies Archives, Culver, Indiana.

Woodcraft—used the various buildings on the Culver campus. The gymnasium, referred to as the "Little Gym," was used by everyone for lectures, theatrical programs, and religious services. Woodcrafters specifically used it for boxing and lectures, and on rainy days, for religious services. For boys who fell ill or got hurt, a skilled nurse and experienced doctors provided care in a modern and well-equipped hospital. The beautifully designed mess hall, built on the main campus in 1911, was a state-of-the-art dining facility that fed all the campers from 1912 through 1916. During those years, the Woodcrafters had their own dining section. Campers ate at tables headed by a camp instructor. Sit-down, country-style meals—with white tableclothes, plates, and utensils—were served by waiters who brought food to each table. However, as the camps continued to grow it

Inside the dining hall. Tables were set for "family-style" meals, with white tablecloths and proper dishes and utensils. Courtesy of the Culver Academies Archives, Culver, Indiana.

became impractical to serve everyone at the same time. In 1917 a large mess tent—on the site of Culver's present day Naval building—was erected to feed the Woodcrafters. With its translucent walls and ceiling, overhead mantel gas lights, and the same beautifully appointed tables found in the mess hall, the woodcraft campers were provided the same sit-down meals they enjoyed in the mess hall.

Woodcrafters' mess tent, with it's translucent walls, circa 1917. Courtesy of the Culver Academies Archives, Culver, Indiana.

A TYPICAL DAY
IN CAMP

Dan Beard surrounded himself with capable assistants, and as a result the Woodcraft camp was recognized as an organized learning experience. In 1912 the campers were placed into four groups called "patrols"—the turtles, beavers, eagles, and rattlesnakes. The group name was changed to "stockade" by Beard in 1913, and *The Culver Citizen* reported on July 17th that there were seven stockades that year—*Blue Raven, Jack Rabbit, Fish, Buffalo, Bear, Red Squirrel, and Red Fox.* Eight boys were assigned to a stockade, and the competition between them was friendly but intense. Beard regularly planned a full day of activities for the stockades that was only interrupted by short recesses, typically after lunch. As early as 1914 and 1915, boys who had previously attended the camp were selected as stockade leaders, an experience that afforded them excellent leadership development.

A busy street at the Woodcraft Camp, 1915. Courtesy of the Culver Academies Archives, Culver, Indiana.

The typical camp day began five minutes before six a.m., when the camp gun was fired. Each stockade had a totem pole where awards—called notches—were registered by red, white, and blue ribbons. The first stockade out of their berth, into their bathing suits, and lined up in the middle of the street, was awarded a notch, while the last stockade to appear was given a yellow ribbon—called a chump mark. While the accumulation of chump marks was certainly a negative by Dan Beard and Woodcraft School standards, among the campers, the boys who earned the most were thought of in another way altogether. Howie Hillis, who had been a Woodcraft camper, and an instructor from 1918 to 1925, recalled Beard's system—

About the only legacy from his time was the badge known as a 'notch'—awarded for an accumulation of merits. There was also a 'top notch.' A part of the legend concerned his system of yellow 'chump' ribbons awarded for the accumulation of demerits. The legend had it that the boys with the most chump ribbons were looked upon by their contemporaries as important figures, if not heroes.

Morning reveille for the stockades was anything but quiet. Each unit of campers was lined up in formation in the middle of the street and put through a series of calisthenics designed to stretch muscles and increase flexibility. Following their workout the boys were marched to the lake to take a morning swim, and then trotted back to camp to lineup for another round of movements—Muldoon's circulation exercises—completed in military fashion. After aerobics, the boys were given the command "bedding out"—which meant gathering up their bed linens and placing them on camp chairs for airing—then ordered to "fall out" to complete the task. After "bedding out," they were given the command "toothbrushes," with each camper taking his tooth powder and brush,

Dan Beard offered the following description of Muldoon's circulation exercises in the August, 1912 issue of *Boys' Life:*

At the command, 'left instep' each scout stooped and put his left hand on his instep, bearing down upon it with his right hand, rubbed it briskly until the command came for the right instep, which was treated in a similar manner. Next they rubbed the right shin, left shin, calves of the legs; then, with the index finger and the thumb, one on each side of their knee caps, they massaged that joint. Next they rubbed briskly the front and back parts of the thighs; then they kneaded the stomach as though it were made of dough; then "slapped a tattoo" on their chests, following this with a brisk rubbing of the right and left arms, after which they rubbed the back of the neck with both hands; then the temples with their index finger.

Woodcraft Camp street. Woodcrafters lined up outside their tents awaiting inspection. Courtesy of the Culver Academies Archives, Culver, Indiana.

Woodcraft class; examining plant specimens and recording findings. Courtesy of the Culver Academies Archives, Culver, Indiana.

rushing to the iron spout from which an artesian spring flowed, and brushing their teeth. Finally, the boys were commanded to dress. When they came out of their tents in their camp uniforms, they lined up for inspection. Following the review, the stockades were marched to the mess hall for their morning meal.

After breakfast, the boys were separated by stockade and put to varying activities under the guidance of instructors. One group would be taken on a plant hike to collect specimens that each boy would then examine and record his findings in a notebook. Other stockades would be instructed in bird-lore, woodcraft and camp craft, as well as first aid, forestry, and the identification of harmless and poisonous snakes. During the first weeks of camp, afternoons were spent carving and painting totem poles, and upon their completion the pole became the symbol—bear, buffalo, rattlesnake, etc—for their stockade. There were also swimming lessons and open swimming at the pier, as well as a wide range of sports—boxing, shooting, track, tennis, and baseball. Distributed on Saturday evenings at the Council Fire were awards for competing in meets, games and tournaments and for completing the requirements for bronze, silver, and gold medals.

As often as possible, the boys were taken on overnight camping trips into the woods surrounding the Academy. On these treks, and during day hikes, a stockade would be responsible for cooking lunch. During hikes and overnight excursions each boy eventually learned how to light a fire and cook. Evenings during camping trips were also filled with rituals of storytelling, campfire pageantry, and the wearing of special uniforms depicting frontier scouts, buckskin men, and Native American Indians. At the end of the day, as darkness settled, tired but happy Woodcrafters retired for the evening.

Finally, a week at camp was made complete by religious services, held outdoors on Sundays. But if the weather was bad the Woodcrafters gathered in the Little Gym. The school took a non-denominational approach to religious experiences for the campers, with services led each Sunday by pastors from different congregations.

CAMP ACTIVITIES

I n 1912, when the Culver Summer School of Woodcraft was established, it purposefully aligned its educational mission with the goals and objectives of the new Boy Scout Movement. Teaching boys to use their hands and their heads was fundamental to Beard's and the Academy's instructive principles. An early promotional catalog stated—*the boy who learns manual training in a well-equipped shop, where every sort of tool is at hand, gains a certain skill without much resourcefulness.* So at the heart of the learning experience of Woodcrafters attending the Culver summer camp was skill and confidence-building resourcefulness. The camp was established with the purpose of teaching boys how to make things with as few tools as possible—a camp axe and jackknife—and with the intent of preparing them to know how to survive and be self-reliant in the great outdoors.

The opening of the Woodcraft school, Beard's role within the Boy Scouts of America, and the initial campfire with rituals of comradeship intended to bond the boys together, were all duly noted in the July 11, 1912 issue of *The Culver Citizen*—

> *With Mr. Dan Beard, National Scout Commissioner of the Boy Scouts of America and America's chief writer for boys on how to do things, the new school of Woodcraft is encamped along the east road and their quaint costumes and novel salute mingle with naval blue and the cavalry yellow of the other schools. Forty boys* [thirty-six actually attended in 1912] *are having the time of their lives as Mr. Beard's protégés. On the opening night of the school all who had reported went through the mythic rite of initiation and put their nostrils to the beaver scent so as to become woodsmen forever. The late comers were initiated at a grand campfire on Saturday night. In the mean-while the members had decided around the council fire that no rule of old men and new was to exist and had chosen crafters for the five offices* [sic]*. At this Saturday night campfire these were solemnly inducted into office by Mr. Beard; their old names were discarded and new bestowed, names that cause any boys heart to leap. Johnson now answers to the call of Daniel Boone, Crapo of Simeon Kenton, Reeves of Kit Carson, Boardman of Davy Crockett, while Richards is yet unnamed. According to tent location, Woodcraft Camp is divided into four stockades; the turtles, the beavers, the eagles and the rattlesnakes and there is keen rivalry among the bands.*

Dan Beard was vigilant in securing qualified instructors, and providing careful supervision for each of his campers. Under his personal direction, Woodcrafters learned to make things, were taught by the best outdoorsmen in America, and experienced all

Dan Beard conducting a class, 1914. Courtesy of the Culver Academies Archives, Culver, Indiana.

that the outdoors had to offer. Guiding the Culver woodcraft activities were many of the projects showcased in Beard's *American Boys' Handy Book,* first published in 1882. This book and other writings had made Beard a household name and had secured his reputation as an innovative youth leader. His *Boys' Life* article from August, 1912, offers a glimpse into how he used the handicraft skill of totem pole carving to engage the boys—

> *My camp was divided into four patrols; each patrol had its own totem pole, while the combination of the four totems made the big totem pole for the camp itself, a gorgeous affair with a blue rattlesnake surmounting it, neatly coiled under the head of an eagle, the latter roosting upon a blood-red beaver and all springing from a United*

43

Woodcrafters, in 1915, pose with their staves—poles that were used for measuring, sports, and, when joined together, became flagpoles. Courtesy of the Culver Academies Archives, Culver, Indiana.

States shield. It must be remembered that when these boys first landed at the Woodcraft camp they were nice and soft, a lot of mama's boys as were ever let loose upon an unprotected country.

During the first weeks of the summer school Beard took the boys on hikes and overnight camping trips to prepare them for their first level of achievement—to become a "Trailer." He also supplemented camp activities with visits and lectures by nationally recognized outdoorsmen. Among the guests during the summer of 1914 was famous explorer, Dillon Wallace; noted author and lecturer on Indian customs and lore, Dr. Charles A. Eastman,

44

known by his native name Ohíye S'a (pronounced O-HI-ye-sa-a); and the first basketball coach at the University of Wisconsin, Dr. James C. Elsom. One of the parents watching Beard with his son commented to Culver's Superintendent Gignilliat *that...certainly this great boys' man has a knack of making instructive things interesting.*

Beard's activities-driven training program grew over the four years he was affiliated with Culver. By 1915 there were ten categories of instruction—fish, birds, forestry, camping, swimming, gymnastics, track, boxing, dancing, and academic studies. Boy Scouts in attendance were encouraged to earn merit badges, and the most popular ones completed by campers were forestry, handicraft, cooking, camping, swimming, first aid, and stalking—now called tracking.

> The 1912-1915 qualifications of a Woodcraft School "Trailer" included—turn in notes on five birds, lay a fire and light it with one match, show efficiency in making a bed and cleaning up a tent, improvise a drinking cup—known as a noggin, learn a set of calisthenics, memorize a set of health rules to govern eating and drinking, show how to stop bleeding and how to bandage ordinary cuts, know the history and composition of the flag, recite the Preamble to the Declaration of Independence, identify and give a fair description of ten plants—including poison ivy and sumac, and recognize and describe five trees.

Forestry, Fish, and Birding

Instructors, such as Captain J.S. Crawley, guided the boys on adventures that introduced them to the natural world. Each morning Crawley took a patrol on a plant hike across the forest lands of the Culver estate. These excursions provided firsthand opportunities for the boys to study northern Indiana trees, shrubs, and wildflowers. They gathered plants, examined them, learned to know them by name, and then supplemented their hands-on experiences with information packed in the pages of Gifford Pinchot's *Primer of Forestry*. The morning hikes began before dawn and breakfast was cooked on route over an open fire.

Other camp leaders helped the boys recognize fish species in Lake Maxinkuckee, and taught them flyfishing and baitcasting. An aquarium set up on the Culver Academy grounds allowed campers to closely watch the behavior of fish. Beard wrote about their fish adventures in the August, 1913 issue of *Boys' Life* –

> *We had a permit from the game warden to use a seine in Lake Maxinkuckee and by this means we were able to secure specimens of all varieties of fish inhabiting these waters. Some of these we preserve for our museums, most of them we release; but the smaller we save for a fine, big aquarium made under my directions for the camp. I only wish that all the Scouts could be as happily situated as my chosen forty . . . You should see them in the water drawing that seine. If the fishes had ears there wouldn't be one on our side of the lake. The boys yell loud in their excitement to catch them.*

In addition to their forestry lessons and investigations of fish, the campers were also taught to recognize birds common to northern Indiana. Instruction happened on field trips and each boy was responsible for keeping a bird-lore notebook.

Hiking and Overnight Camping

Overnight camping was a highlight of the Woodcrafters summer experience. Beard and his staff of outdoor instructors believed

Woodcrafters hiking to the River Camp at Ora, 1913. Courtesy of the Culver Academies Archives, Culver, Indiana.

that overnight trips beyond the confines of Culver were important for breaking-up the monotony of daily routines. Beard was an expert in all that pertained to life in the wilderness, and was a master at teaching camping skills. And, even though the great woodsman was sixty-two-years-old in 1912, he was still fit and still able to hike and lead overnight camping trips. Beard described a good woodcrafter as *someone who has the ability to use the things he would find around him.* His list of camping lessons included— the selection of a campsite, and

1912 Woodcraft Camp catalog. "Making improvised Beds of Brush." Courtesy of the Culver Academies Archives, Culver, Indiana.

47

Daniel Beard and two Woodcrafters at an overnight campsite. Courtesy of the Culver Academies Archives, Culver, Indiana.

planning its layout and drainage; setting up tents and shelters; locating a water supply, purifying the water, and disposing of it. Other instruction involved selection of clothing for outdoor camping, proper camp utensils, how to make a camp bed, how to address health concerns and provide first aid, how to set up a campfire for heating and

One of the camp instructors had a dog named "Taps." The boys loved him, took him on their hikes, and swam with him in Lake Maxinkuckee.

A lesson in fire building and camp cooking. (Dan Beard and Lieutenant Beard are sitting at the right of this group. Courtesy of the Culver Academies Archives, Culver, Indiana.

The Woodcrafter is not considered a real cook until he can flip his flapjack in proper style. Courtesy of the Culver Academies Archives, Culver, Indiana.

cooking, how to read the weather, and how to do basic land navigation. Beard also taught the campers how to build a fire in the wet woods from materials found there using just one match.

The Woodcrafters made the first of many overnight camping trips to the Tippecanoe River on August 19, 1912. This particular nine-mile hike was typical of their camping adventures. While the boys carried their overnight necessities, an equipment wagon transported required camp accessories. Beard carefully selected their campsite by the river. The Woodcrafters were energized by their lunch of fried ham and potatoes, cooked over an open fire, and accompanied by hot cocoa. For the rest of the afternoon the boys explored the river's edge and surrounding countryside. At dinnertime, a hearty supper satisfied their hunger; and then, tired from their long hike, the boys hit the hay for a good night's sleep. An early morning breakfast sustained them for recreational activities, and after lunch everyone prepared for the journey back to Culver.

Aquatic Skills

In addition to the woodcraft skills the boys acquired on their overnight camping trips and on hikes, Lake Maxinkuckee also offered them the opportunity to master aquatic skills. All the boys were taught to swim, and for those who were new

1912 Woodcraft Camp catalog, "Shoot the Chutes." Courtesy of the Culver Academies Archives, Culver, Indiana.

Swimming lessons were conducted at the pier, using "corrals" to which boys were harnessed for safety while they learned to swim. Courtesy of the Culver Academies Archives, Culver, Indiana.

The swimming pier also included several "Chutes" where boys enjoyed the fun activity of shooting down a very tall sliding board into the water. Courtesy of the Culver Academies Archives, Culver, Indiana.

learners, special devices were used to suspend them in the water. The suspension harness was also used to practice swimming strokes. Proficient swimmers took advanced instruction in swimming and diving. Boy Scouts were encouraged to earn their merit badge for swimming. Popular activities on the swimming pier included "shoot the chutes"—sliding board, swinging rings, water polo, and diving from the towers. All the swimmers, no matter their level of skill, were carefully guarded by the pier officer and his assistants. Dan Beard was proud to say, *"No boy left camp without knowing how to swim."*

Movement and Athletics

U nder the direction of skilled instructors from the Culver Secondary School, all the boys learned to dance—the one-step, the two-step, and the waltz. They were also taught gymnastics— tumbling and vaulting, they participated in track and field meets, and they were also given boxing lessons—with an emphasis on self-defense.

Handicrafts

W ith the theme of "learn by doing", and with a focus on the teaching of pioneer skills, the Culver Summer School of Wood- craft offered a unique oppor- tunity for campers to acquire

1912 Woodcraft Camp catalog, "Building a Canoe." Courtesy of the Culver Academies Archives, Culver, Indiana.

useful handicraft skills. Camp leaders believed a boy would become a well-rounded man if he learned outdoor living skills—like reading trail signs and understanding Indian gesture language, and if he acquired useful hand skills— such as handling and using a belt axe and a jackknife. Each summer, experienced outdoors men taught the boys the fundamentals of woodcraft along with highly prized handicraft

A handicraft is a useful or decorative object made completely by hand or with simple tools— such as an inexpensive pocket knife, safely carried and easily sharpened.

A wide range of materials— such as wood to create a totem pole, leather to make a pouch, or feathers and fabric to design an Indian headdress—are used in the making of a handicraft. Many different skills are required— such as woodworking, leather work, and sewing.

Handmade work and handicraft skills were highly valued in the early 20th century.

skills. While most handicraft lessons were held outdoors—in formal classes as group projects or on field trips—beginning in 1913 when it was raining, the boys took their training in a log cabin designated for handicrafts. Instruction included kite and boat building, craft ing bird shelters, boxes, roosts, and swallow boards, as well as the design and execution of bridges, dams, shacks, shanties, shelters, camp torches, and camp ovens.

A group project that served as an early bonding activity was the carving of symbolic stockade totem poles, a custom that helped the campers improve their carving skills while also getting to know and to identify with their fellow stockade members. On field trips and overnight hikes the boys learned the skill of whittling—carving with a knife—turning good soft wood, such as pine and willow, into simple tree limb whistles and such animals as rabbits, dogs, and horses. Over the years, the School of

Woodcraft and handicraft skills being taught by Captain James H. Beard (Daniel Beard's nephew), with Dan Beard at far right with other instructors, 1912. Courtesy of the Culver Academies Archives, Culver, Indiana.

Woodcraft maintained enthusiasm for handicrafts by introducing new ones and deleting those no longer of interest.

Academics

Academic instruction was not mandatory, but for those who needed or desired traditional coursework, most of the Culver Military Academy faculty—a corps of some thirty instructors— were available during the summer. While they were primarily there to work with the boys in the Naval and Cavalry summer schools. They also offered classes to Woodcraft campers. The subjects available to the boys included—arithmetic, mental arithmetic (calculations performed in the mind without writing down figures or using a calculating device), elementary algebra, English grammar, English composition, United States history,

Greek history, Roman history, civics and government, Latin, German, and French for beginners, public speaking, reading, writing, and spelling.

A study tent for the Woodcrafters was located at the southern end of the camp. When instructional classes were not in session the tent was used for study time. The campers' academic records were kept in the office of the Culver Academy headmaster, and his staff spent the last two days of camp preparing statements of credit to be carried back to the home schools of the campers.

Training for Scoutmasters

While there had been a two-week program for Boy Scout troop leaders in 1912 at the School of Woodcraft, in 1915 the Culver Military Academy announced that a complete training course for Scoutmasters of the Boy Scouts of America would be offered that summer. The two-week program, held August 2nd to 16th, was led by Chief Beard and Capt. James H. Beard—Dan Beard's nephew—Officer in Charge of the Woodcraft camp. With the mission and purpose of using the Woodcraft camp as the focus of study, lectures and demonstrations were provided around a curriculum that included the history of the Scout move-ment, evils Scouting was attempting to correct, Scout activities— such as tasks required to earn merit badges and games appropriate for Scouts, and the conditions to be met to become a Tenderfoot, a Second Class Scout, and a First Class Scout.

Chief Beard, in speaking of his vision for the Scoutmaster program and his enthusiasm regarding its value to boys, to the Boy Scouts Movement, and to American society, commented—

"*. . . that there were 9,000,000 young men in the United States eligible for the Boy Scouts and if enrolled under the Boy Scout banner would constitute such a powerful organization as to make any nation think twice before tampering with our national honor or safety. Consider 9,000,000 physically fit young men so trained as to be able to take good care of themselves, bow to discipline, and educated to be good men, lead useful lives, and do good deeds, and animated by the virtues of good men.*"

The Scoutmasters program also captured the attention and interest of the Boy Scouts of America leadership. Among those who visited and offered lively conversation during the 1915 training weeks were Chief Scout Executive James E. West, and Scouting Organizer Samuel Moffat.

AWARDS

An award system at the School of Woodcraft gave campers the needed incentive to participate in camp activities and competitions. Their medal was a beaver—master of woodcraft in the animal kingdom—encircled within the elongated "C" of Culver's logo. During the four years Beard led the school, campers were rewarded by levels of achievement—bronze, silver, and gold medals—when they met the requirements of increasingly difficult standards.

The bronze "C," called a "Notcher," was a medal worn on the front of a camper's service hat. This award was given as soon as a camper had learned basic woodcrafting skills. When a boy mastered the benchmarks for this award, he was identified as a "Trailer." The silver "C," called a "Mid-Notcher," was a belt buckle, and was awarded for the accomplishment of more difficult tasks. The boy who earned silver was known as a "Ranger." The gold

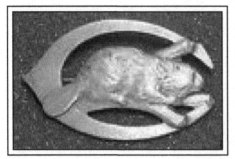

The bronze "C" pin, referred to as "The Notcher," and worn on a camper's service cap, was awarded to boys who mastered basic woodcraft skills. Source of image is unknown.

"C" was the most difficult award to achieve. It was called a "Top Notcher," and the boy who met all the assignments for this award was called a "Guide," and the badge he earned was worn on the shoulder of his shirt.

The only information about Culver "C" awards earned in 1912 is from an August 22nd article in *The Culver Citizen.* The reporter noted that *four campers had earned a silver "C."* But there is no mention of anyone meriting the gold that year, or of those who won the basic bronze. Information for 1913 and 1914 was more complete. In 1913, forty-nine campers earned bronze, twenty-seven met the requirements for silver, and nine achieved gold. And in 1914, sixty-four boys merited bronze medals, while fifty-one earned silver, and nineteen were awarded gold. In addition to the tasks required for Woodcrafters to earn "C" awards, there were also athletic and aquatic

In 1912, requirements for the gold "C" included: building a bird house, sketching three birds and identifying their differences, cleaning and cooking a fish, improvising a camp light and bed, making a fire without a match, understanding the fundamentals of advanced first aid, knowing how to inspect for good drinking water, showing knowledge of mosquitoes and the diseases they convey, steering, caring for, and repairing a boat, demonstrating how to rescue someone from drowning, providing the names and principal achievements of two distinguished citizens of your state, passing a general quiz on plants that included their locales and uses, reading a map and making rough sketches from field notes, and, finally, identifying fifteen trees and explaining how trees are propagated, enforced, and planted.

Campers displaying their stockade totems at an awards ceremony, 1915. Courtesy of the Culver Academies Archives, Culver, Indiana.

competitions throughout the summer—tennis, baseball, track and field, water polo, swimming and diving, as well as angling and boating. While these events were held for all three summer schools—Naval, Cavalry, and Woodcraft—rivalries were kept between the boys within each particular school, and their competitions were supervised and guided by directors with specific activity experience.

Awards were distributed by Dan Beard on Saturday evenings when Woodcrafters assembled at the Council Fire. This weekly activity was a highlight of the camp experience, and parents and visitors were invited. Following the lighting of the fire, Woodcrafters marched in, squatted in a circle, and then several campers entertained the audience with woodcraft skills and stunts. A reporter with *The Culver Citizen* wrote about the first Council Fire in the newspaper's July 25, 1912 edition, noting that the event included *building of the fire, sign language, report of officers, kicks, initiation, the woodcraft oath, stunts, talks, stories, and songs.*

The original Council Fire Ring, 1915. The Woodcrafters sat on tree stumps while guests sat in the stands. The actual location of the first Woodcraft Camp Council Fire Rings at Culver is unknown, but in 1917 a permanent site was established for the weekly ceremony. Courtesy of the Culver Academies Archives, Culver, Indiana.

Council Fires were ceremonial events to which officers arrived dressed as frontiersmen, where older campers were initiated as "Buckskin Men," and the younger ones as "Leather Stocking Boys." It was also where the talents of campers and leaders were showcased. Dan Beard was a storyteller known for his tales of famous American pioneers and frontiersmen. Guest instructors entertained with other kinds of performances. One visitor especially popular with the campers was Ohíye S'a, of the Santee Dakota (part of the Sioux tribe), and of English and French descent. A personal friend of Beard's, Ohíye S'a was a writer, lecturer, and political reformer who worked on behalf of Native American rights. He was also known as Dr. Charles A. Eastman from his years as a Boston University-trained physician. At

Woodcraft campfires, dressed in full Indian regalia—complete with war bonnet, Ohíye S'a told stories of Indian folk lore, Indian dances, and shared his knowledge of the trail and field. Since 1912 Indian lore has been an important part of the Culver Summer School of Woodcraft.

Further details of Council Fire activities were recorded in an August 22, 1914 article in the *Vedette,* the Culver Military Academy's newspaper—

Council fires began in 1912 with Dan Beard telling pioneer stories and spinning yarns about American folk heroes, like Davy Crockett and Daniel Boone.

It is not known for certain where the first Council Fires were held, but with the rapid growth of the Woodcraft Summer School, in 1917 an area was developed to hold the first permanent council fire ring.

In the years following, changes and additions were made to the Council Fire activities, to include the addition of Indian lore and dances.

The weekly council fire held on Saturday night contained many of the things taught by Dr. Wallace. The first thing shown was the putting up of a "dog tent" by the Eagles and the Owls, and the cooking of camp bread, flap-jacks and 'darn-goods' by the Wolfs and Owls. Next in order came axe throwing, in which little Mercer tied Ross, the hero of all other axe contests. Axe throwing became the chief sport in camp, with matches gone on every day, and there was much rivalry among the best throwers. Then a show called 'The Feet of the Young Men' *was given by the Raccoons and Peccaries, for which they got fifteen stockade ribbons. Dr. Wallace then bade good-bye to the woodcrafters and Dr. Eastman, dressed in the garb of an Indian chief of the Sioux tribe, gave a talk. Last, came a funny and interesting talk about cats and dogs by Captain Crawley.*

While the awards distributed and the events of the Council Fire evenings inspired the boys to do their best, the campers' admiration and deep respect for Dan Beard—who maintained his position as their "Chief" by always wearing his white buckskin suit when he was with them—was well acknowledged during the ceremony at the final Council Fire of 1912. That evening the campers awarded their beloved leader with a Loving Cup. Overwhelmed by the gesture, Dan Beard remarked—

> *"Hit me with a club and I would know how to come back at you. Throw a brick and I would know how to answer you. But when you begin to throw bouquets, I'll confess that I do not know what to say. I will say, however, that I am moved by your gift and I will say that you have given me the best vacation I have ever had."*

At the end of the first year of the Culver Summer School of Woodcraft, Chief Beard exclaimed, *"I had the time of my life."* More than 100 years later, Council Fires remain a tradition, and are now held in an area at the Culver Military Academy known as The Council Ring.

THE SUMMER SCHOOL OF WOODCRAFT: THEN AND NOW

aniel Carter Beard and his family spent all eight weeks at the Woodcraft camp in 1912, but for each summer from 1913 to 1915 he was there for only two weeks. Beard's nephew, Captain James H. Beard, was in charge when Dan Beard was not there. Capt. Beard managed the program with the assistance of officers who were added according to Culver's apportionment of one leader for every sixteen boys. At the end of 1915, Dan Beard found family responsibilities and commitments to his publishers and the Boy Scouts of America too pressing to return for another year. Additionally, he was not entirely happy functioning within a military environment, was irritated by the Culver administration's trimming of activities he saw as essential, and, most significantly, was planning his own outdoors school. In 1916, on land he owned in Pike County, Pennsylvania, Dan Beard opened the "Outdoor School for Boys."

Following his resignation in 1915, Beard recommended Dillion Wallace as his replacement at the Culver Summer School of Woodcraft. A lawyer, writer of boys' fiction, outdoorsman, and world traveler, Wallace was known for his expeditions exploring Labrador, Canada, first in 1903 with Leonidas Hubbard, and again with his own teams in 1905 and 1913. Wallace's 1905 book, *The Lure of the Labrador Wild,* chronicled the 1903 expedition and was a best seller. His outdoors exploits made him an excellent choice for Culver. Indeed, during the years Dan Beard led the camp Dillon Wallace was a frequent visitor who also gave several lectures. Like Beard, he too was described as a *boy's man,* and Wallace had his own ideas about woodcrafting—

> *Woodcraft training makes a boy self-reliant, observant, and considerate. He not only learns to care for himself but to think of others. Patriotism, promptness, courtesy and service are the cardinal principles preached in the Woodcraft camp.*

The Culver Summer School tradition continues to this day. More than 1,300 campers from around the world arrive each summer to learn leadership skills and improve personal self-confidence. Today's Woodcraft camp—a six-week, all-activity experience—attracts 600 boys and girls, aged nine to fourteen, each year. And while nature and cultural pursuits are an important part of present day camplife, there is also the opportunity to select from eighty electives intended to enhance academic and athletic competence.

The relationship between the summer schools and the Culver Educational Foundation remains strong today. Over the years, many

Woodcrafters have matriculated and graduated from there. For many, the Woodcraft program represents the best of Culver—lessons taught, leadership cultivated, and lots of personal attention.

Information about the Culver Educational Academy summer schools is available on their website at www.culver.org/summer.

These are the qualities for which the Academy summer school programs are best known, and what the schools are all about.

PART TWO

THE DAN BEARD
OUTDOOR SCHOOL FOR BOYS
1916–1938

1916 - building day for the trading post.
Courtesy of Dan Beard's 1917 outdoor school promotional catalog.

There was no place in the outdoor school that was as special and revered as much as the Saturday Evening Council Fire area.

Edward Dodd

TESTIMONIALS

During his four years directing the Woodcraft Camp at Culver, Dan Beard dreamed of having his own Woodcraft Camp. His mind went back to Lake Teedyuskung, where he owned approximately twenty-seven acres of lakefront property and had built a two-story, four-bedroom log cabin. He thought this summer and weekend retreat would be ideal for a woodcraft camp. In the summer of 1916, the "Dan Beard Outdoor School for Boys" was established. The school-camp was designed around the woodcraft, handicraft, nature study, and patriotic programs of his articles and books for youth. His leadership pioneered the areas of camping, physical fitness, character building, patriotism, and purposeful recreation. The Outdoor School became widely known after its first few years. Magazine advertising-especially in *Boys' Life*- and Beard's own articles and books, along with word-of-mouth, helped promote the summer camp. The influence Beard and his instructors projected upon the impressionable youth of America, at the time, was immeasurable. A closer, more intimate, study of the influence of the school can be made by studying personal letters written to Beard, magazine articles, and personal interviews with campers, camp employees, and instructor/counselors, about the Outdoor School

Edward Dodd, an avid environmentalist and creator of the *Mark Trail* comic strip, was an instructor and Beard's "Officer in Immediate Charge"

Edward Dodd, who was also a teacher of outdoor lore and advocate of conservation, had worked at Beard's camp for thirteen summers. Under Beard's guidance, he sharpened his writing and illustration skills. In 1946, Dodd's "Mark Trail" comic strip debuted in the The New York Post in which the character urged his readers to avoid environmental carelessness such as littering, vandalism, and harming wildlife.

Today, Mark Trail, with nearly twenty-three million fans, is the official character of the National Oceanic and Atmospheric Administration (NOAA), representing the National Weather Service and NOAA Weather Radio.

during the early 1920's. A personal friend of the Beard family, he had firsthand knowledge of the Outdoor School and of Beard's personality and habits.

"A great boy's man, an egotist who could be petty on rare occasions. An opportunist, colorful romantic and dramatic. An Artist who was great with drawing animals. His greatest contribution was his love and enthusiasm for the outdoors and 'mother nature'." He challenged boys 10 to 18 years of age to lean woodcraft because it develops the intellect and body at the same time. He was in his mid-seventies when I ran the day-to-day camp operations. His son Bartlett was my assistant and when I moved on Bartlett because the camp's top officer. The "Chief," as Dan liked to be called, knew all the campers by their first name and was ready to assist them with woodcraft and handi-

craft projects. Many of his campers went into outdoor professions. The campers all loved and respected their "Chief" and I saw many with tears in their eyes when they had to say good-bye after eight weeks in camp."

One of the instructors who was also a leader of a stockade at the Outdoor School, in 1916 and 1917, discussed "The Chief":

"He was personally very clean, extremely honest and allowed no alcohol or tobacco in camp. He was very thoughtful of others, made it his business to know every camper personally called them by first names-or a nickname-went on overnight hikes with the campers and saw that each one was sheltered and well-fed. I remember on one overnight hike I saw him share his supper with a boy who did not do a good job of cooking his supper. An excellent teacher-not only as a lecturer, but in showing them himself. At times, I think he exaggerated in some of the stories he told-but not often. He installed the idea that if you wanted to do something bad enough you could do it. He often said, 'take the can out of can't and do it'."

In her review, Elizabeth Chisholm, of *The Red Book*[1] magazine wrote:

"This is indeed a 'School of the Outdoors' and not a recreational summer camp. Dan Beard is an excellent leader and opens up, in a way that only he can, an entirely new and fascinating world to the boys in his care. Nature lore,

---

1 *The Red Book* - a popular women's magazine that later became *Redbook Magazine*. It moved from print to a digital-only format in 2019.

practical woodcraft and camp craft are taught in a manner
unequaled in any camp I visited.

Axe throwing, archery, handicraft, knot tying, tree grafting,
fire building and many other pursuits of the American In-
dian and the pioneers are among the activities. The boys
make their own bows and arrows and knife cases and
build all types of log cabins and other primitive struc-
tures. Swimming, canoeing, hiking and horseback riding
are among the athletic activities. Military drill and tent
inspection is held every day. Simple living modeled after
the American pioneers and made more appealing to the
modern boy by the use of colorful Indian symbolism, Boy
Scout virtues and loyal American citizenship are stressed.
The entire camp is divided into stockades, eight boys to
each, and the boys work for the honor of their stockade as
well as individual honors, which is a fine point.

The Dan Beard School of the Outdoors is a unique institu-
tion and one that really develops boys physically, mentally
and spiritually. We can, of course, recommend it enthusi-
astically."

Victor Aures, an instructor under Beard during the years 1916-
1917, explained:

"Dan Beard (The Chief) was an extrovert had a good
sense of humor—was always in good spirits—he was
fair minded—dedicated to service for others-loved people
and animals, was interested in the arts and most
patriotic. I was always grateful for my association with
him. He also helped my career as an artist."

Aures also related that he was the stockade leader for Howard Hughes, Jr. (age ten) in 1916 and again in 1917 for Howard and his cousin Dudley. Howard achieved the status of a "Buckskin Man" at age ten, but in December of 1916 returned the badge awarded to him, confessing that he had violated the Buckskin Oath by eating some candy. This demonstrates the reverence in which the campers held their "Chief." Howard was eager to get back to the familiar rustic setting of Chief Beard's camp during the summer of 1917 with his friend Dudley. Beard's son, Bartlett, who was one year younger than Howard and Dudley, became close friends with both boys. Howard's overprotective mother asked Beard, via a letter, to pay attention to her son's health. When Howard returned home that summer Mrs. Hughes wrote to Beard:

> "He is in better condition, I think that he has ever been. His cheeks are round and fat and rosy and he is full of 'pep'. We think you are largely responsible for this and hope he can be with you next summer."

Howard's mother also wrote directly to Lieutenant Aures. One paragraph read:

> "I am afraid you will find him pretty nervous this year. He was so much improved in that respect by last year's camp that I hoped he was outgrowing it and his super-sensitiveness but it seems to have all come back this spring since he has not been well. That is one reason I was particularly glad for you to have him in your stockade. I think you understand him well enough to help him over the many times he gets his feelings hurt . . . If you can help Howard

to take the teasing without getting hurt and resentful we will surely be lastingly in your debt. Dudley makes friends so much more easily than Howard does and Howard feels that keenly too . . . If you can help him to forget himself, get along better with boys and perhaps teach him to keep his hut in order, I ask for nothing else."

Howard came back to visit the Outdoor School on several occasions in the 1930's.

A Chicago, Illinois, mother praised Beard for sending a written opinion of her son instead of a percentage grade. She noted that, *"It indicates a closer personality touch and a more intimate acquaintance between teacher and pupil."*

A Kingston, Pennsylvania, mother told of her ears burning because of the tales her son had been telling since arriving home. She noted, *"We knew all the camp yells, and all about the distinguished men guests of the summer, the good table you set, etc."*

On their return from England, an Allentown, Pennsylvania, family wrote Beard about the improvement of their son, "The camp life has certainly made him look upon school-camp duties at quite a different angle than before."

Another father from Saginaw, Michigan, wrote,

"We certainly appreciate the work your school did for Bob during the summer for he is a very much improved boy. The training he received is something that I do not believe he could have received in any other way, and, to my mind, it is the logical way to train a boy and develop those natural instincts which are too often overlooked."

Physical training was designed to improve posture, stimulate growth, and increase strength and flexibility by the end of the eight-week term. One such letter commended Beard and expressed grand appreciation:

> *"I want to tell you I have never made a better investment for the money paid you for James' term with you this summer. You not only furnished him with a delightful two months, but gave him a store of ideas, thoughts, and experiences which continue to delight him as the weeks go by. Physically you did him a world of good and in addition made contributions to the development of his character, of which we get pleasing evidence nearly every day. The one wish of James and his parents is that there may be more summers which he can spend in the same way."*

Beaumont Whitton was both a Boy Scout and junior leader at the Outdoor School from 1927-1929. During this time the school was at its peak and accommodated close to eighty boys for eight weeks. Whitton discussed Beard and the Outdoor School:

> *"'Chief' was a great advocate of a man physically capable of taking care of himself. Autographed in the front of a book he gave me is a statement, 'Woodcraft is the ability to live anywhere and to live well even alone.' I feel Beard felt that very strongly. He was a great admirer of the mountain men who opened up the mountains of the west and did a lot of beaver trapping. The 'Buckskins', of which I was a member, were an honorary organization of campers and quite an honor to be taken into. The Buckskins had a high moral code and a code that was intended to impress one with the idea of physical ability, the ability to take care of himself honestly, thoughtfulness to others, all the better*

traits that would make a man complete. It was the ideals and the ideals of the officers who attended the camp that made such an impression on me. I was only seventeen to nineteen years old and had been a Boy Scout for five years or more and it was impressive to me to see grown men giving consideration to these things. I feel most boys that attended this camp felt this influence and to me it would mean that this impression of high moral code was a major contribution the D.B.O.S. made to the schools. I valued highly the three summers in Pike County as they were a great importance in my development."

Dan Beard and Ed Dodd discussing camp activities
courtesy of Special Collections Department, Pullen Library, Georgia State University

FROM NEW YORK CITY TO THE GREAT OUTDOORS

he Beard family moved to Flushing, New York, in 1870. Dan, who was working as a land surveyor back in Kentucky, followed his family in 1878. Being artistically talented like his father—the well-known portrait painter, James H. Beard[2]—Dan pursued a career as a commercial illustrator. He and his brother, William Henry "Harry" Beard, also an illustrator, shared an office in New York City. There they worked as cartoonists, sketch artists (drawing on the spot at the scene of fires, accidents, and other emergencies), and illustrators for pamphlets, book and book covers-including those written by the celebrated American author Mark Twain, best known for his books about *Tom Sawyer* and *Huckleberry Finn*.

---

2 James H. Beard (1812-1893) was an accomplished 19th century portrait artist. Born in Buffalo, NY, his family moved to Ohio, where he honed is artistic skills. In 1846 he returned to New York and his work began to get noticed. In 1870 he moved his wife and children to New York, permanently, and his career flourished.

> I n one of Mark Twain's letters to Beard, he wrote:
>
> *"What luck it was to find you. There are a hundred artists who could have illustrated any other book of mine, but there was only one who could illustrate this one. Yes, it was a fortunate hour that I went netting for lightning bugs and caught a meteor. Live forever."*

Like many ports of entry in the late 19th century, New York City found itself a city on the verge of explosion—with a population growing every day with the arrival of immigrants from Europe and beyond. Fascination with the outdoors and the desire to "get back to nature" was a result of increasing reliance on modern technology and conveniences, as well as a desire to escape the crowded city life.

As both an artist and an outdoorsman, Beard had keen observation skills, and watched both children and adults carry out their lives in the crowded, dirty, metropolitan environment. The city, at that time, did not adhere to its tenement reform laws, allowing for unsanitary conditions that affected the health and welfare of poor immigrants. Food was purchased at unclean open-air markets, with fish laid out on boards in the heat of the summer, and where vendors spit on apples to shine them for sale. Many boys came from battered, broken homes and lived on the streets. Commonly called "street boys," they caused trouble and formed neighborhood gangs. Complicating these matters, there were no child labor laws, and children as young as six years old worked twelve-to-sixteen hours per day for little pay, to help support their families.

During this same time, the country was beginning to feel the surge of unrestrained prosperity, which allowed many people the luxury of escaping to the country. This period of about thirty years was known as the Progressive Era.[3] Social reform, prohibition, and women's suffrage were all taking shape. Tourism and recreation grew out of the movement, and camping was popularized by the YMCA, the Chautauqua movement, youth service organizations like Beard's *Sons of Daniel Boone,* and other social groups. Fascination with the outdoors and the yearning to "get back to nature" was due to an increasing reliance on modern technology and conveniences, as well as the desire to escape the crowded city life.

Not far from the smothering metropolis were boundless areas of woods and trout-filled streams and lakes. Many New Yorkers looked to these areas

Camping was a key part of many youth organizations that used it to teach both self-reliance and team-work. In 1905, Beard served as an editor of the magazine, *Recreation.* To help promote the magazine, he founded the organization "Sons of Daniel Boone" for boys, to encourage their interest in outdoor recreation. It later became "Boy Pioneers of America."

The Boy Scouts, which began in England in 1907 and quickly spread to the United States, was also founded on the core principle that outdoor adventure, camping, and woodcraft/handicraft were an important part of a boy's moral development. In 1910, the Boy Pioneers of America, along with other similar scouting groups, became incorporated into the Boy Scouts of America of which Beard served as the organization's first national commissioner. Having merged his groups with the Scouts, he founded what was to become the oldest, continuously chartered troop in the United States—Troop #1 of Flushing, New York.

Beard, himself, became an Eagle Scout at the age of 54.

---

3 The Progresive Era (circa 1890-1920) - Progressivism in the United States was a broadly based reform movement that reached its height early in the twentieth century. Historically it was the advocacy of social reform; philosophically, it was based on the idea of progress, asserting that advancements in science, technology, economic development, and social organization are vital to the improvement of the human condition. The primary objectives of the Progressive Era included purification of the government at all levels, modernization, a focus on family and education, prohibition, and women's rights.

for an escape. It mattered little whether it was fishing, golfing, hiking, or finding solitude; it was simply about breathing fresh air and experiencing the great outdoors. Like many other enthusiasts, Beard began surveying these nearby lands for a weekend retreat and place to spend his summers. For several years the young artist, illustrator, magazine editor, and conservationist explored different locations within a day's travel of New York. He was anxious to return to nature and the similar surroundings he had enjoyed growing up in Ohio and Kentucky, and sought the most remote, wooded area, near water that he could find in order to enjoy his great love of fly-fishing.

Land Purchase

In 1887, Beard and his brother Harry purchased two wooded parcels of land totaling twenty-seven acres near Hawley, Pennsylvania, in the Pocono Mountains. Approximately 130 miles from New York City, the two properties, which were adjacent to one another, had approximately 500 feet of lake frontage on Lake Teedyuskung. Beard bought Tract One which consisted of 19.85 acres, with Harry's land (Tract Two) consisting of approximately 7.16 acres.

This wilderness area—rich in the Native American tradition that Beard so loved—consisted of a clear blue lake filled with a wide variety of fish; plenty of deer, and red and gray foxes; virtually every species of

Lake Teedyuskung, also known as "Big Tink Lake," was named for Indian Chief Teedyuskung (1700-1763), a spokesman of the Susquehanna Delaware Indians. Teedyuskung in the Indian language means "he who makes the earth tremble."

bird found in the American northeast; and an abundance of hemlock trees. Beard often commented that the land was *"nature without a shave, a hair-cut, or a manicure."*

When Harry died unexpectedly, in November, 1889, he bequeathed all his holdings to his parents. In 1905, after Beard's mother, Mary Carter Beard, had passed away, Beard and his two sisters, Adelia and Mary, inherited Harry's tract of land.

Then, in March, 1916, Beard and his sisters entered into an agreement to deed Harry's property to Beard for use in the development of his new camp called the "Dan Beard Outdoor School for Boys," which opened in the summer of 1916. For many years Beard envisioned using his land for this endeavor.

A third tract of land, consisting of eight-hundred feet of lake frontage, was purchased by Beard in 1926-about ten years after the camp opened. This acreage, across the lake from the original Beard properties, was used to expand the Outdoor School. It was called "Buckskin Cove," and was primarily used for overnight camping trips. To get there, the campers used canoes to transport their food, tents, and overnight gear across the lake.

"Wildlands"

Once the land was purchased, Beard immediately got to work building what would be the first of three log cabins to stand on the site. He enlisted the help of his friend James Johnson, with whom he would often hunt and fish, as well as a group of lumberjacks from Maine. Together, these men built "Wildlands," a huge, two-story, four-bedroom cabin, complete with a sleeping porch overlooking Lake Teedyuskung. The building was described as

Wildlands, the author's log house in Pike County, Pa.

Drawing by Dan Beard
Courtesy of Bear Mountain State Museum

"the first real log cabin after the pioneer era ended." This became Beard's weekend retreat, vacation home, and studio. Here he could relax during the summer, far from the noise, dust, and heat of the city. It was a place where he and Johnson, as well as friends from the *Camp Fire Club of America*, in New York City, would spend most of their vacation time fly-fishing on the lake.

THE "CHIEF"
AND HIS VISION

Beard was known as "Uncle Dan" to millions of men and boys through his involvement with the Boy Scouts, and before that with the *Sons of Daniel Boone* and *Boy Pioneers*. He diligently promoted the values of trustworthiness and responsible citizenship, as an author of many outdoor books, and for his monthly articles in *Boys' Life* magazine. But at his outdoor school, he preferred to be called "Chief."

From 1912 to 1915, he conducted the Summer Schools of Woodcraft at the Culver Military Academy. While at Culver, he made a careful and exhaustive study of how to organize and supervise a woodcraft school. He felt certain that the methods used there were safe, sound, and educational. The popularity of the programs were validated by the fact that the number of thirteen-and fourteen-year-old campers increased from thirty-six to 140 during the four years he was there. and although he was in charge of the Woodcraft Camp, there still were limitations as to what he could and could not do. On top of that, the living accommodations for his family, the climate, and the camp's "overly disciplined" atmosphere was wearing on him. So with the encouragement of his nephew James, and other friends, along with his desire to start a camp of his own, Beard decided to leave Culver at the end of the 1915 season to set up his own camp.

The "Dan Beard Outdoor School for Boys" officially opened in the summer of 1916, with the plan to offer both summer and winter sessions; the summer school furnishing recruits for the winter school, and vice versa.

The summer school ran for eight weeks, from the end of June through the middle of August, and focused on woodcrafts, swimming, camping, physical fitness, and academics. The winter program—that was held for one week after Christmas—focused on snow-shoeing and cross-country skiing, ice skating, skate sailing, tracking, and cold weather camping.

Beard directed and supervised these school-camps[4], and employed his own carefully planned system of discipline, instruction, and play. He was assisted by his devoted family and competent staff. In many of his writings, he believed that an education in woodcraft was of significant value, and in its broadest sense, was even more important than a high school or college education. He wrote that it-

---

4 Beard used the term 'school-camp' to describe his enterprise because it was a progressive educational experiment-an extension of the schools that were developing during the Progressive Era of American Education.

". . . develops the intellect and body at the same time, while scholastic education alone, too frequently develops only certain functions of the brain in an abnormal manner, with no reference to the body. The finest men in history were all trained in the open. It has taken years to convince the people that the outdoors is intended by God Almighty for playground, living space, bed-chamber and school."

The Outdoor School was the only civilian-run school to employ 'military-like' order and discipline. Every day the boys were put through formation drills to teach prompt obedience; physical exercise to develop their bodies, and stringent inspections of both person and living quarters.

The objectives of the school were derived from standard educational principles, patriotic values, and good citizenship, and focused on physical training, environmental knowledge, and woodcraft activities. Beard described these objectives in his promotional pamphlets.

"To build the boys up physically, mentally and spiritually, and on this establish a foundation for abiding belief in honor, sportsmanship, truthfulness, America and the creator; as also to ground the boys in essentials of right living; to train them to be leaders, that this generation of boys may be better American citizens in every respect than the one preceding it. The Dan Beard Outdoor School does not rely on precedents; it is here to establish them. It holds sacred only those things of yesterday which tend to promote advancement in morals, culture and physical strength, for tomorrow."

Dan Beard, wife Allie and daughter Barbara, on the front porch at "Wildlands"
courtesy of the Daniel Carter Wing scrapbook collection

ESTABLISHING THE OUTDOOR SCHOOL

sing his own lodge and properties in Pennsylvania, Beard opened "The Dan Beard Outdoor School for Boys." He used his own name for the school because of its fame and reputation. Plus, it carried a great deal of influence and support—both of which were necessary for obtaining the financial backing the camp needed. Beard trusted this combination would guarantee success from the start. He believed that as soon as the school had the proper buildings and equipment, it would become widely known and, as a result, would be financially sounds. Fortunately, friends from the *Camp Fire Club* donated large amounts of money and materials needed for the school's success.

In each year's annual report, Beard paid tribute to the *Camp Fire Club*. He also recognized other important people who helped make the camp the success that it was—old comrades, his legal

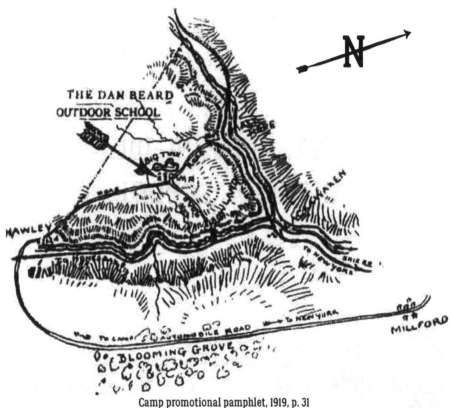

Camp promotional pamphlet, 1919, p. 31
Courtesy of Liberty of Congress Manuscript Collection

counselor, offices of the corporation, his advisory committee, and the generous friends who provided endowment funding. These men loaned their names and influence to the Outdoor School because they believed in Beard and the work he was doing for the boys of America.

In the first year's annual report, he noted:

Shortly after opening the camp, Beard incorporated the entity as "The Dan Beard Camp, Inc.," though it was still referred to as "The Dan Beard Outdoor School for Boys."

Athough he was hesitant about taking such a leap—business-wise—he knew it was essential for securing the funding needed to run the camp.

It wasn't that he doubted the success of the camp, but rather because of his own reluctance in handling other people's (investors) money, as well as having to solicit funding and issue company stocks.

The Camp Fire Club of America was organized in 1897 to bring together hunters, anglers, explorers, naturalists, and individuals who subscribe to the principles of adventure and fellowship in the great outdoors, and to further the interests of sports afield and wildlife conservation. The Club had many notable members, including Boy Scouts of America founders Daniel Carter Beard and Ernest T. Seton, and conservation giants Gifford Pinchot, 'Buffalo Bill' Cody, and Zane Gray. The organization functioned with a focus on the preservation of the natural environment, habitat, forests and wildlife preservation through the Camp Fire Conservation Fund (www.campfire fund.org).

The club's most significant environmental efforts of the 19th and 20th centries included: saving the American Bison in 1905, passing the Fur Seal Preservation Act in 1909, the founding of Glacier National Park in 1910, and passing of the Plumage Bill in 1910.

The Camp Fire Club, located in Chappaqua, N.Y., continues to support conservation through a variety of efforts nationwide and globally.

"The Camp Fire men launched our Outdoor School in order to educate the boys that they will, if I may be pardoned for using a paradoxical expression, love hardship for hardship's sake, or more correctly speaking, love it for the sake of stirring adventure, and because they have a contempt for mollycoddles.[5] Physical hardship is stimulating and brings to the front our best qualities."

Building the Camp

Beard was fortunate to have his nephew, James H. Beard, to assist him with the camp. In addition to being the second-in-charge, James was responsible for all the supplies and transportation. His experience working in refuse camps[6] along the flooded deltas of the Mississippi River proved a valuable asset to the Outdoor School.

---

5 "Mollycoddles" - boys who are used to being pampered or "coddled."

To get the camp functioning, a number of essential services and structures needed to be built or installed. With barely thirty days to work, James and a team of local craftsmen dug a thirty-foot well; built a spacious, thirty-by-sixty foot mess hall pavillion with an adjacent kitchen; store houses for goods and supplies-to include an ice house; constructed a water tank, lavatories (with plumbing), and wash rooms—all in accordance with approved sanitary plans.

Other buildings and structures needed before any of the campers, faculty, or staff arrived, included:

- bunk houses for campers and staff
- living quarters for the kitchen staff
- a swimming pier and boat house
- a meeting tent for rainy day activities
- a council fire area for camp ceremonies.

Thanks to the engineering skills of James, and the hard work of his men, the Outdoor School was ready by the middle of June-a full two weeks before camp was to begin.

Staffing the Camp

Starting a new business venture is stressful and exhaustive, and can be quite a difficult undertaking—especially for a business

---

6 Refuse camps were temporary camps built to house displaced persons or families for short periods of time and to provide basic human needs. Often included in these building projects were the construction of roads, levees, canals (to divert water), and the general clean-up of flooded areas. These were cooperative ventures between the Federal Government and the affected state(s) or region(s).

James Henry Beard' was like a son to Dan Beard. But his actual father was Dan's brother, James Carter Beard. (Carter was their mother's maiden name.)

James ("Jamie") played a very important role in Dan's camps. At Culver Academy, he was second-in-command of the Woodcraft School, and held the title of "Captain."

When Dan left Culver to start his own camp, James followed, and again became the second in charge. Unfortunately, James was only there for the first summer. Having been drafted into the Army in 1917, during World War One, James was seriously injured in a gas attack in France and never returned to the camp.

that requires so many employees to be available at the start. The 1916 camp staff of instructors, tutors, counselors, and support staff (medical and dental personnel, mess hall staff, and administration), had to be assembled within a few short months to take charge of the camp and ensure the well-being of the campers. Beard was fortunate to find experienced and capable men who were up for the challenge. Among those who joined the staff were:

- James H. Beard - Dan's nephew and Second-in-Charge. He helped set-up and build the camp.

- Dana A. Barnes, who came over from from Culver -was an instructor of Indian sign language, Native American legends, and snake lore. He taught at the Boston Technical School (now the John D. O'Bryant School of Mathematics and Science).

- Victor Aures, of Buffalo, New York - a veteran of Beard's youth groups- *The Sons of Daniel Boone* and *Boy Pioneers*-taught nature lore. He was also a Scoutmaster, well-versed in Boy Scout ethics, woodcraft, and wilderness handicraft, making him an excellent instructor.

- Robert L. Beard (no relation), another former instructor from Culver - was put in charge of discipline and also taught signaling and Morse code.

- George P. Yocum - in charge of the swimming pier at the lake, as well as the swimming instructor.

Of all his dedicated staff, Beard's most valuable asset was his wife, Alice. She entered into the school's work with great enthusiasm and dedication. "Allie," as she was known, took charge of the kitchen and meals, ensuring everyone ate well.

Her ability to stand steadfast as a defender of the boys on many occasions was noted. At times she was a "mother" to boys who were homesick or not feeling well. She was always available if a camper needed a female figure to talk about bullying, outdoor fears, fear of the dark, and writing letters-as the boys were required to write home weekly. She also served as a "sounding board" for her husband, and influenced him in many ways.

In his autobiography, Beard wrote:

> "As I look back over the years I see how fortunate I was that Mrs. Beard married me. We have had a splendid time. She has been with me on my trips into the wilds, she has aided me in my Scout activities, she has stood behind me in all that I have done. Her common sense has steered me from many a possible shipwreck."

Budgeting the Camp

Beard hoped to attract between eighty and one-hundred boys the first summer. However, starting a camp from scratch with minimal help, limited advertising, and time constraints, proved to be a monumental task so he revised his expectations and limited enrollment to only forty boys (forty-one boys actually attended). Of this reduction in attendance, he rationalized *"fewer campers would allow for more individualized attention and personal instruction for the boys."*

Edward Seymour, camp treasurer, projected the first year's budget on the attendance of 100 boys, at a cost of $200 each (today's equivalent of around $2000). Based on these numbers, and with camp expenses totalling $16,046, he anticipated a profit of close to $4,000 (about $40,000 today). But because costs to build the camp were more than expected, and enrollment was limited to only forty boys, this profit was reduced significantly.

The camp barely supported itself the first year. With all the initial expenses, and the mounting payroll costs, Beard knew he had to make a number of changes in order to keep the school afloat. So, to keep the cost of attendance reasonable for the boys, and still earn profit, he took less of an income, and Mrs. Beard offered her own car for camp use so a vehicle did not need to be purchased right away. After the first summer, they also decided against bringing back professional waiters to serve the dinner meals, as was the tradition at Culver. Although there was no scrimping on food or equipment, Beard believed that professional waiters were a costly and unnecessary luxury. Instead, Mrs. Beard supervised the dining hall, and the camp's college-student counselors and the leaders of each stockade served the meals.

Maintaining and Improving the Camp

Camp improvements continued as needs were identified. Additional lodging and activity facilities were built for the boys and faculty as the camp expanded. By 1918, Beard realized that an officers' quarters adjoining the mess hall was necessary so that someone would be on hand at all times to guard the provisions and supplies, as waste and theft were becoming a problem. The front porch of the new addition was used as a meeting place for parents and guests. The rear area contained bedrooms, a washroom, toilet facilities, and a storage room for officers' trunks, wardrobes, and personal items. Using leftover construction materials, a shed was built to store the campers' trunks and personal items while they were at the school.

In addition to the officers quarters, a number of other buildings were added to the camp over the years. Oftentimes, these buildings were constructed by the instructors and campers themselves. They included:

- two more log cabins and a wood frame cabin
- a trading post
- a barn with stables and a corral
- a small library building

Annual maintenance ensured that the camp would remain a healthy, clean, and safe place for both camper and staff. Each spring much the same work necessary to prepare the camp for its initial opening had to be redone to ensure the camp met all health and safety standards. These tasks included:

- inspecting roofs and making necessary repairs
- setting up tents and living quarters for
  campers and staff

- cleaning of brush and leaf debris from around buildings and on camp streets
- re-erecting the meeting tent
- repairing, or replacing, if necessary-the swimming pier from damage caused by ice during the winter
- re-anchoring the floating swimming platforms in the deeper part of the lake
- repairing or replacing benches on the tent platforms and around the camp
- regrading the roads and walkways with shale
- replacing worn-out row boats and canoes.

THE FACULTY OF THE OUTDOOR SCHOOL

1917 Outdoor School faculty.
Sitting: Daniel C. Beard, the "Chief"
Standing: Captain James Beard, Victor Aures, George Yocum, Dr. Finck,
Dr. Long, Robert Beard (no relation), Dana Barnes, Mr. Long

Courtesy of Daniel Wing's scrapbook

A key to achieving success is to assemble
a strong and stable management team.
Camp is my happy place.

Camp confessions: (LCMC)

MARKETING THE CAMP

orty-one boys from thirteen states attended camp the first summer. Although admission was open to one hundred boys, attendance fluctuated between thirty-eight and seventy-eight boys over the camp's twenty-two year history.

Promotional pamphlets and advertising for the summer camp stated, "... *only boys who can remain the full period of the course* (eight weeks) *will be admitted.*" However, because of low enrollment during the early years, exceptions were made. A letter to one boy's parents mentions such an exception,

> "*We have enrolled the maximum number of pupils this year; but owing to his mother's illness, one of the boys is leaving on the first of August and we will, therefore, have room for your boy. The tuition for . . . the month of August would be $100.00.*"

An image from the 1922 Outdoor School for Boys promotional catalog.

During the off-season, admission for the next summer was solicited by recruitment letters and advertisements in various publications such as *Boys Life*. Letters were sent to prospective campers' parents, emphasizing the advantages of the Outdoor School:

> *"Your name has been given us . . . for literature and information concerning the Dan Beard Outdoor School. Owing to the coal-less days, etc., the engravers have been unable to make the cuts for the catalogue, so it will be another two weeks before our booklet is ready for distribution. However, we have placed your name on our mailing list and shall take greatest pleasure in sending you a copy just as soon as same is ready.*
>
> *In the meantime, here are a few facts which I hope will help convince you that ours is the school for your son."*

By 1928, of the seventy-three boys in attendance, thirty-six were recruited from advertisements in *Boys Life* alone, with the remainder coming from ads in other publications and returning campers—many of whom brought a friend with them.

During the winter of 1928-1929, inquiries for the summer camp totaled 633.

Summer Camp was about growth and accomplishments, it was the counselors job to help these things happen not to just keep the kids busy.

Camp Confessions: (LCMC)

THE CAMP AND THE
WAR YEARS

eard was sixty-six years old when he opened his camp. He believed he had another four or five good years left in him for the strenuous work required of running an outdoor school. After this, his plan was to have James take over the school. Sadly, though, James was severely injured in the War and unable to return to the camp. Because of this, Beard remained in charge until his son graduated from Syracuse University in 1930 and took over full-time. Bartlett had attended both the Culver Woodcraft Summer School and the Dan Beard Camp each summer since the age of five. He became a counselor at the camp while still in high school and continued in this role throughout his college years, teaching nature study, horsemanship, and marksmanship.

Because of Beard's age, his duties would be limited primarily to the administration and organizational planning of the camp, reviewing staffing needs and skills curriculum (to include woodcraft and handicraft skills), purchasing new equipment, and creating the camp's brochures and advertisements. He also provided oversight of the landscaping and the yearly clean-up, maintenance, and structural repairs. And always with an artist's eye, he constantly looked for ways to add artistic, dramatic, and other aesthetically-pleasing touches to the camp to make it an interesting learning environment.

All of the physical work was to be done by the younger men on the faculty. However, the manpower drains of World War I, once the United States became involved in 1917, took away many of his experienced counselors, doctors, nurses, and laborers. James and several of the other key instructors also left for military service, leaving only Beard and a skeletal staff to shoulder the responsibilities of the school. Beard described the challenges of running such a high-caliber operation with minimal staff:

> " . . . it included the work and details of a summer hotel combined with the all-important recreation and school program, and had not Mrs. Beard volunteered her services and taken charge of the mess hall, thus doing away with an expensive steward and the necessity of a clerk to watch the steward, we scarcely would have staggered through the depressing period of the war."

In the summer of 1918, the boys, like many other young people their age, participated in the war effort by selling thrift stamps to visitors at the school. Profits went toward the needs of the camp and its ongoing improvements.

There was a two-year, post–war recession immediately following the end of the World War I, lasting from January 1920 to July 1921. The economy had begun to grow, but it had not yet shifted

During World War I the United States government used thrift stamps as a means of financing the war effort. In order to meet the growing financial demands of the war, the Treasury Department sold approximately $21 billion worth of Liberty bonds to encourage thrift and support. Because many people couldn't afford even the smallest bond—valued at fifty dollars—the Treasury Department issued Thrift Stamps and War Savings Stamps.

Thrift Stamps were twenty-five cents each, and once sixteen were collected, they could be exchanged for War Savings Stamps, which carried a four percent interest that compounded quarterly and were tax free. These were primarily targeted at school children and immigrants. Public school teachers helped to promote the stamps as a way to teach children the values of patriotism and saving. The campaign began on January 2, 1918, and closed at the year's end. The Treasury Department paid five dollars for each War Savings Stamp when they matured, on January 1, 1923. In that short period of time, the Treasury Department raised over $1 billion dollars.

from a war-time economy to a market-driven[7] economy, which handicapped the growth of the school during that time. However, despite the recession—and even the pandemic of the Spanish flu (1918-1920) the school continued to grow, and by 1927 attendance had almost doubled. Bartlett Beard, remarked, *"1927 was the peak year for the camp . . . , with seventy-eight boys in attendance."* He believed that having an even larger number of boys was unrealistic, as it would compromise on the quality of the training.

Beard said of this milestone—

"We will probably never reach our goal of one-hundred boys. Not too many at a time, for one of the real secrets of my success is that I am always personally in touch with every boy in my school and seventy boys is about all I could be 'Daddy' to during one session."

---

7 Market-driven economy - An economic system in which decisions and the pricing of goods and services are guided by the interactions of individual citizens and businesses (supply and demand) with little or no government intervention.

Can you be my counselor next summer?
is the ultimate compliment.
Camp Confessions

You don't need permission to do something great..
Camp Confessions

CAMP LEADERSHIP

eard admired the good order and discipline practiced at Culver Academy, but he braced at being micro-managed and constantly questioned by twenty-something lieutenants: *"I don't want to take advice or orders from any shaved-faced young lieutenants."* Nevertheless, he organized his Outdoor School in the same manner as at Culver, dividing the boys into small groups known as "stockades," and assigning military ranks to the leadership.

Stockades were similar to a military squad, and each one had it's own leader. Each stockade was composed of eight boys and a leader, who was usually an older boy who had previously attended camp, or one of the college students who served as camp counselors during their summer breaks. Instructors were given titles equivalent to military officer ranks, and the boys were expected to address their leaders accordingly.

Upon arriving at the school,[8] each boy was assigned to a stockade with its own totem pole. Just like at Culver, during the first week of camp each stockade would carve and paint their own heraldic totem animal (such as an eagle, bear, badger, etc.), and mounted it to the top of the poles. These totems identified each stockade.

The rank structure was limited to just a few levels of leadership. Dan himself was called "Chief," which would be the equivalent of a military "Colonel." The camp's "second-in-charge" was a "Captain," and the instructors and other key figures were given the rank of "Lieutenant."

Leadership at the camp changed from summer to summer, but the steadfast Beard always remained in charge. The first summer's leadership team consisted of "Chief" Beard; "Captain" James Beard; and "Lieutenants" Victor Aures, Dana Barnes, Robert Beard, and George Yocum.

Beard had planned to turn over the management of the camp to his nephew, after five years, but when James didn't return to camp following his wounding in World War I, Beard continued to run the camp for another thirteen years. In 1930, after his son graduated from college, he took over running the camp.

Bartlett ran the camp until 1934, with his sister Barbara managing the administrative aspects of the operation. The Outdoor School was the main source of income for Bartlett and Barbara during those years, with Dan maintaining his income from *Boys' Life* and book royalties.

---

8 Many campers traveled by train to get to the Outdoor School. They would have been picked up at the stations in the towns of Lackawaxen, Mast Hope, and Rowlands, Pennsylvania.

"DAN YOU'RE A CHIP OFF THE OLD BLOCK" DAN BEARD AND HIS SON DANIEL BARTLETT BEARD AT PIKE CO. PA. ABOUT 1931.

Courtesy of Bartlett Beard

Bartlett wrote:

"In 1930 I took over full-time, summer and winter, on the camp as the 'Chief's' assistant, or virtually as director, spending the winters recruiting, preparing booklets, writing advertising and promotional letters, etc. The Depression was in full swing and the camp had fewer and fewer boys. In the fall of 1933, my wife and I had very little money. In fact, we lived on macaroni and cheese for two weeks. We got $50.00 per month from the camp and my wife's parents sent us $25.00 per month. My family furnished us a cabin on their property at Suffern, New York. I got a job as a foreman in a C.C.C. camp which I stayed with until the end of winter in 1934. I got about $140.00 per month—we were on easy street! I left, preparing to go back to the Dan Beard Camp, but didn't see how we could manage it financially, so I accepted a job as a wildlife biologist with the National Park Service and made my career with that agency. My sister had married a scout executive, but shortly after I graduated from College (1930), she got divorced. She then worked with us on the Dan Beard Camp and continued after I had to desert. The camp's facilities were in bad shape, enrollment was down and finally the camp closed in 1938 when my dad was eighty-eight."

It is unknown who ran the camp from 1935 until it closed in 1938.

ADMISSIONS, TUITION, UNIFORMS AND EQUIPMENT

amp instructors and counselors believed that boys between the ages of ten and eighteen could attend the camp. Occasionally a boy of nine was admitted after Beard interviewed his parents. And although the camp was endorsed by the Boy Scouts of America, the camp was not limited to scouts only.

Tuition the first year was $200.00 per boy, but with reduced number in attendance, and reduced revenues, the school was barely able to support itself. As a result, it became necessary to make changes to the price of tuition and equipment.

In 1916, the cost for uniforms and equipment was $35.00, which was included in the fee. However, In 1917, those costs were not included in the price of the camp, and the boys paid an extra charge of $27.00 for their uniforms and kits, bringing the total cost of attendance to $227.00. In 1918, the cost of camp had risen to

$250.00, plus the extra charge for uniforms and equipment. By 1920, tuition had increased to $300.00, plus the extra fee; and by 1931, tuition had reached $310.00 for the eight weeks.

Each camper was responsible for purchasing two uniforms– a utility uniform for every day wear, and a more formal one for dinner and special events– as well as their equipment kits. These kits contained: a jacknife, belt axe, guard rope, canteen and mess kit.

The daily school activity and hiking uniform included an olive drab (O.D.) long-sleeve shirt; olive drab shorts called "flappers;" a service hat (similar in style to the cover worn by a Park Ranger or military Drill Instructor); long khaki stockings (knee socks) cuffed at the top; and tan leather hiking boots.

The dress uniform was similar to the utility uniform, but made of a higher quality fabric, and was a slightly different color green. It included a red bandana, which was tied around the neck, and an O.D. green overseas cap-like that which was worn by World War I soldiers. It was worn for personal inspection, evening meals in the mess hall, and all day Sunday.

> The uniforms at Culver Academy were designed by the Culver administration with input from Beard. The uniforms the boys wore at the Dan Beard Outdoor School were ordered from the Sigmund Eisner Company of Red Bank, New Jersey—the same company that made the official Boy Scout uniform.
>
> The Sigmund Eisner Company was a uniform manufacturer, and, at the time, the largest manufacturer of uniforms in the United States. Having contracts with both American and foreign governments, they made the uniforms worn by servicemen during World War I. And by 1922, they were the exclusive manufacturer of uniforms for the Boy Scouts of America.
>
> Additionally, Sigmund Eisner was the great-grandfather of Michael Eisner, who was the CEO of The Walt Disney Company, from 1984 to 2005.

Cap, right side

Cap, left side

This uniform—the formal uniform—belonged to a camper who attended the Outdoor School for several summers. The cap shows the various awards this boy earned during his summers at the camp. The five white circles, about the size of a quarter, with red crosses centered in them are called "Top-notch" awards. The six-pointed star is the "Theodore Roosevelt" Top-notch award; and the large circle with the rounded Native American Sun Wheel ("Swastika" represented the "Knowledge" award. It would have been impossible to earn all the awards shown on this boy's cap during a single eight week session. See page 149 for more information about Outdoor School awards.

The dress uniform, as described by Bartlett Beard:

"The uniform gave the campers a trim and picturesque appearance. The O.D. shirts, with the sleeves neatly rolled up, the O.D. shorts or "Flappers" displaying the bare knees, the O.D. stockings rolled down with a cuff at the top, and the tan colored shoes, made a charming uniform for the boys to which the service cap added a finishing touch."

Other clothing items that were required were: an outdoor sweater or jacket, a pair of overalls, walking shoes, and a poncho for wet weather.

Most campers came from wealthy urban families. In case of suspension, dismissal, or voluntary withdrawal, no part of the tuition-which included room and board-uniforms or other expenses was refunded.

In the Indian subcontinent's Indo-Ayran Sanskrit language, the word Swastika is composed of two words, "Su" (good) and "Asati" (to exist) meaning, "May good prevail."

At the Dan Beard Camp, the Swastika represented a camper's knowledge, and symbols borrowed from Native American lore were used to promote the American Indian's role in frontier America. It was chosen to represent a "whirling log," which symbolized "a healing ritual."

The first Scouting use of the "Swastika" was for the "Thanks Badge" introduced in 1908 by Scouting's Founder, Lord Baden-Powell of England. It continued to be worn world-wide in different forms until 1935, and was seen as a symbol meaing "Good Luck."

World-wide Scouting discontinued the badge in 1935 because Adolph Hitler adopted the Swastika as the emblem of the National Socialist Party of Germany, thereby degrading this once innocent symbol of honor.

Today, it is negatively associated with Nazi ideology, White Supremacy, and Anti-Semitism, and is considered one of the most controversial and hateful symbols in the world because of the horrors associated with it.

HOW THE CAMP
WAS SET UP

he Outdoor School was well-situated in the forest of the Pocono Mountains of northeast Pennsylvania. Once the home and favorite hunting grounds of the Delaware Indians, the campers lived in a rugged outdoor setting in an area surrounded by rolling mountain terrain and dense forests with shale covered dirt roads leading into the camp. In his March 1926 *Boy's Life* article about his visit to the camp, Bertram Broome, an illustrator and author who wrote fictional stories about the American Southwest wrote:

> *"There in the beautiful setting of hills and lake is the Dan Beard Outdoor School, the only one of its kind in the world perhaps, and in its teaching of morals, self-reliance, wood-craft, swimming, scouting, character-making and building, it stands as a permanent monument to Mr. Beard whose ideals are of the highest."*

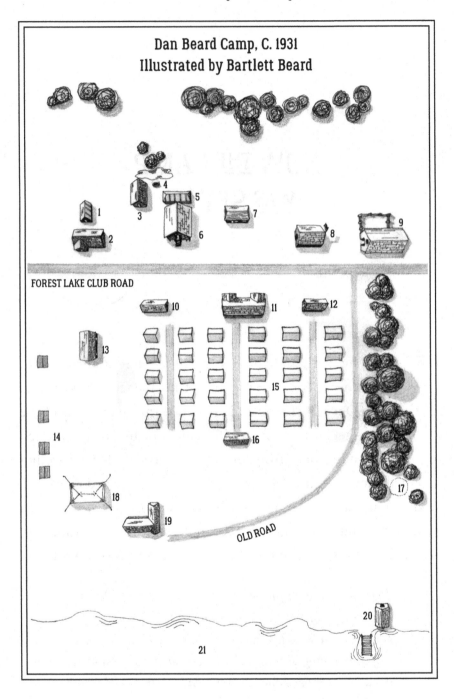

Dan Beard Camp, C. 1931
Illustrated by Bartlett Beard

FOREST LAKE CLUB ROAD

OLD ROAD

MAP LEGEND

1. Frame Cabin	12. Counselor's Cabin
2. Dan Beard's Second Log Home	13. Wash House
3. Ice House	14. Pit-Priveys
4. Well	15. Tents
5. Storage Cabin	16. Open Front Cabin
6. Mess Hall	17. Council Fire _ Ceremonial Ring
7. Chief's Quarters	18. Hospital Tent
8. Library	19. Dan Beard's Original Log Cabin
9. Barn and Corral	20. Log Boat House and Swimming Pier
10. Counselor's Cabin	21. Lake Teedyuskung
11. Trading Post	

The Tents

Similar to Culver, living quarters consisted of modified tents with two boys occupying each tent. (Occasionally, with an odd number of campers, three campers lived in a larger tent.) The tents were aligned in rows which gave the impression of streets in a small village. Similar, but larger, living quarters for counselors and instructors were set up along the outer perimeter of the tent area- within an earshot of the boys tents, and nearby was the "Trading Post," where the boys could purchase small necessities and snacks, as well as send and receive mail.

The "boxed-screened" tents were open on all sides, but boarded up halfway, to just above the cots, so there was a constant flow of air but no draft on the boys as they slept. Each tent also had a screen door to keep the tent free from insects, and flaps that could easily be rolled down for protection from wind and rain. In the front,

Tents were pitched on platforms, with the tent fly—the entrance flap—roped up to create a shelter area, under which a bench was usually placed. Courtesy of Bear Mountain Trailside Museum.

Initially the boys slept on old army metal cots, but later were replaced by wooden-framed single beds. Courtesy of Bear Mountain Trailside Museum.

the tents were shaded by a tent fly that extended eight feet, providing extra shade and a place for the boys to sit under, outside.

Mess Hall

One of the first Outdoor School buildings constructed in 1916 was the mess hall. Beard knew an important part of a growing boy's life was his appetite. Vigorous daily activities in the open air made for hungry young men who craved and enjoyed good, wholesome food.

The mess hall was a thirty-by-sixty-foot, platformed, screened-in pavillion, designed to seat up to one hundred boys and staff. The kitchen was adjacent to the mess hall and was personally supervised by Mrs. Beard. Each year she hired the kitchen staff, which consisted of four cooks, led by Mrs. Dalton. And during

Mrs. Dalton and her staff prepared a the meals at the Dan Beard Camp. Thanks to her "visitors and boys are lavish in their praise of our food," said Beard. Courtesy of Bear Mountain Trailside Museum.

the first year, professional waiters were hired to serve the meals. They wore traditional white duck jackets, and service was similar to that at a fine hotel. But when that became too costly, it was decided that the camp counselors and stockade leaders would serve the meals instead.

Meals were an integral part of camp life, and Mrs. Beard worked hard to ensure they were both delicious and nutritious. She made up the menus, employed the kitchen help, organized the dining room tables by stockades and saw that all the tables were set properly with white linen tablecloths, napkins and proper silverware. The food was served country-style by the stockade counselors and instructors. Many counselors and officers at the camp felt that Mrs. Beard's interest and preparation of the food was a major factor for boys returning to camp year after year.

Every day the boys would march to both breakfast and dinner by stockade (lunch was often taken out in the field, as the boys would be engaged in various classes and activities), and stand at attention during the saying of grace, and until the order "seats" was given. Once seated, they remained at "attention" with arms folded until the command of "rest" was called and the meal would then begin. The stockade leader and one instructor sat at each table. It was their duty to not only direct the conversation, but also to see that the boys sat properly, used their knife and fork correctly, and ate appropriately. All meals were conducted in a proper and gentlemanly manner. The boys really enjoyed the food, and many wrote home boasting about the "fine eats" they had in camp. Beard believed that the camp's reputation for "serving a good table" had proved to be a better recruiting tool than any magazine advertisement.

After the morning and evening meals, the stockades would line up outside the mess hall and march back to their tents.

Camp Headquarters and Other Buildings

A timber frame cabin, built by campers during the early years of camp, accommodated eight to ten people and was used

Camp Headquarters
Courtesy of Northeast Pennsylvania (NEPA) Council of the Boy Scouts

for stockade meetings and small group lectures. A canvas tent was used as the camp headquarters and meeting area from 1916 to 1925, after which it was replaced by Beard's "second log cabin." With four small rooms in the rear, a stone fireplace, and a wrap-around porch, the 28'x30' foot cabin is the only building remaining from the Outdoor School and has been donated to the Boy Scouts of America. The Northeast Pennsylvania (NEPA) Council of the Boy Scouts plans to move it approximately 15 miles away to the Goose Pond Boy Scout Reservation in Paupack Township, Pennsylvania.

A storage cabin, built in 1918, was referred to as the "Officer's Lodge." Because of its proximity to the mess hall, and the fact that an officer was always on hand to guard the provisions, it was used to store food and supplies. Also in proximity to the mess hall was a cabin known as the "Chef's Quarters" which housed the kitchen staff.

Swimming Pier

The camp's "Lincoln Trail" led to the swimming pier on the lake. The pier, which extended from the shoreline, was constructed of large hardwood planks that were bolted together. On the far end of the pier, located in deeper water, was a diving board (which had a spring enabling the swimmer to bounce off the board) and a stationary diving post (platform) from which the swimmer could jump. Another wooden raft was anchored further out in the lake, and served not as a life-saving device, but as a float or swimming pier, and the advanced swimmers would swim to and dive from it. All aquatic sports and recreational swimming were supervised, from the pier, by two or more lifeguards and one lifeguard in a boat.

Medical Services

A hospital tent, similar in style to the living quarters of the boys, was constructed during the first year of the Outdoor School. It was located in the northwest corner of the camp, near Beard's beloved cabin "Wildlands."

For the first three summers, the school had both a doctor and dentist onsite for the entire eight weeks. Doctor Lawrence Simcox, a well-known physician from Philadelphia, was popular with the boys because he wore the coveted Buckskin Badge and taught the first aid and field sanitation courses. Doctor Harold Pruett, a local dentist, was available to look after any dental issues. Beard said, "we were the first camp to have a dentist available for the entire eight weeks of camp."

After the war, Beard relied on medical students on school break to staff the hospital tent. They also taught the sanitation and first aid courses, the Boy Scout First Aid Merit Badge class, and served on the Court of Honor for the badge.

The Senior Color Guard
Courtesy of Bartlett and Barbara Beard.

Every Boy Learns to Swim
Courtesy of Bartlett and Barbara Beard.

CAMP ACTIVITIES

The theme of the Outdoor School was "Learn by Doing." Beard's contribution to outdoor education and conservation practices was his pioneering endeavors of outdoor activities. His belief was that every boy was born with untold capabilities for creative expression, and that his Outdoor School was a means to harness those abilities and develop lifelong skills, enabling his students to become leaders in the modern world.

Beard wrote:

> " . . . the most successful Americans have been those who have learned the nice adjustment between mental and physical development and who have neglected neither."

Such an education was the goal of the Outdoor School. Beard believed this was best accomplished by general outdoor training in which woodcraft and handicraft were the dominant activities. Counselors and instructors recalled him occasionally teaching a class and "very often would stop and show a camper a better way of doing something." Beard insisted that *"the boys should learn the things they want to learn, and do the things they wanted to do."*

Because Beard believed that the boys at Culver had greatly benefited from individual instruction and attention, one instructor was hired for every eight boys enrolled at his camp. Three hours were devoted each morning to instruction and demonstration during the eight weeks of camp, and campers were never forced into activities they didn't like. Areas of study the boys could choose from included woodcraft, handicraft, camping, lifesaving, first aid, nature study, forestry, construction of survival shelters, cooking, canoeing, crafts (art, leather, and woodwork), archery, foil-fencing, and aviation.

There were, however, some activities Beard felt were essential for the boys to learn. Each boy had to learn to swim build a fire under all conditions of weather and to make a Buckskin shirt, leather knife sheath and drawstring ditty bag (sometimes called a poke).

Learning to whittle with a jackknife was considered by Beard as both essential and a lost art, and was put to practical use. Campers were taught how to properly open their knives and how to cut the wood *away* from their bodies. The boys learned to carve wooden broaches for their neckerchiefs and noggins (wooden drinking cups) from burls[10] sawed from a tree. Other popular items made by the boys were moccasins and beaded quivers for the arrows they made.

Campers were taught to make fire by friction. They had to learn to care for themselves in the woods, pick out the best wood for building fires, cook without utensils, learn to cache food and supplies, build various shelters that were waterproof, construct beds of hemlock boughs, and practice orienteering (which is land navigation without the use of a compass).

In the area of nature study, the boys were taught to follow their own curiosity. The woods surrounding the camp were abundant with nature in many forms. Beard often wrote about the camp setting:

> "Over one-hundred and forty-seven birds of different species visit or live around the camp and forty-five varieties of trees grow there. A hundred and sixteen varieties of wild flowers and about thirty different mammals have been identified near camp."

To be a good woodcrafter, Beard emphasized that a camper should be an outdoor "Sherlock Holmes." He believed the camper should have knowledge of the habits of all the creatures of the woods in order to identify which animal made the signs and markings on the trail.

Beard knew that boys had a natural interest in Native Americans, therefore Indian lore and dancing were also part of camp activities. Frontier Indians were regarded as mysterious and heroic figures. Activities were developed through instruction

---

10 Burls (also known as burrs) are outgrowths or bulges on a tree located near the roots, in the middle of a tree, or sometimes as a ring around the trunk in which the grain has become deformed. Burls, which are usually covered in bark, start out small but can grow large enough for new trees to sprout from them.

on how the Native Americans lived in the woods and on the great western frontier, where their very existence depended on knowledge of woodcraft and archery. Native American dancing, accompanied by drums, bells, and rattles, was encouraged because of the physicality, pageantry, and religious ceremonies associated with the pioneer era.

Swimming

The 1919 camp booklet described swimming as *"an activity which develops a boy's physique, gives him self-confidence, and makes him graceful in action and poise."* Beard believed it was absolutely essential that all the boys learn how to swim before leaving the Outdoor School. To ensure that they put in the maximum effort, each of the three camp awards had swimming as part of the test. In order to pass his first degree, a boy *"must be able to swim fifty-feet."* Before he could pass the second degree, he *"must be able to dive correctly",* recover articles from the bottom of the lake, and swim at least two-hundred yards. And before he could pass the third degree, he *"must demonstrate"* the ability to rescue a swimmer from drowning.

Beginning swimming was taught near the lake's shoreline, where it was shallow. A plunge at 5:30 a.m., as an eye-opening morning bath, followed by a recreational swim in the afternoon, ocurred each day. All boys not excused for medical reasons were required to take part in both morning and afternoon swims. Canoeing was another popular activity, but was only offered for boys who could swim 300 feet. In 1920, a nine-year old boy was admitted to camp. The normal age for admission was ten, but a Dr. Green of Easton, Pennsulvania assured Beard that his son, E.M. Green, could hold his own with the older boys. Young Green was an excellent swimmer and fulfilled all the requirements for a Woodcrafter. He also won the only

Swimming awards that were earned and worn on the camp uniform included a Bronze "B" pin for swimming one mile, a Bronze "B" for swimming three-hundred feet, a "Silver DBS" for swimming one mile and "Gold DBOS" for swimming three miles.

DBOS swimming award for his three-mile swim, which had never been awarded until he attended in the camp's fifth year. Green earned the award by swimming along the shoreline of the lake and its indentations. The young camper was in the water two hours and twenty-eight minutes and suffered no ill-effects. A boat with two lifeguards and his father followed alongside him. This feat was a precedent and Green was envied by all the campers. He was awarded by Beard at the weekly Saturday evening Council Fire Ceremony and received a standing ovation.

Overnight Camping Trips

After Beard bought a parcel of land across Lake Teedyuskung from the Outdoor school in 1926, older campers were given opportunities to go on overnight camping trips. They would travel by canoe or rowboat to "Buckskin Cove."

This overnight camping trip into the "wilderness" was designed to give the boys a firsthand learning experience with natures. Usually eight to sixteen boys went on the camping trip and all tents, supplies, and equipment had to be transported to the campsite. The boys slept in two-man tents or in the open air and were taught how to prepare their own meals. One of Beard's famous sayings was, *"a fellow who cannot throw a flapjack is sadly lacking in the skill one expects to find in a real wood-crafter."*

During the day, the boys were entertained with treasure hunts, hikes, trailing skills, burling excursions (cutting wood from the outgrowth of a tree trunk or branch), and instructed

L ake Teedyuskung is fed through several natural springs that offer clean drinking water.

Because the campers had access to one of those springs on the property and the fact that it was also accessible to hikers, fishermen, and picnickers, it had to be cleared of any natural debris and covered with a roof. A pipe was used to carry the water approximately thirty-feet to the lake's shoreline where the boys would set up camp. Beard felt this action was necessary to keep the spring from becoming polluted because the overnight camping trips taken to this area across the lake relied on this fresh water supply.

in plant, bird, tree, and insect identification. One of the highlights of this overnight excursion was when the instructors, counselors, and sometimes Beard himself, would have the boys prepare the campfire around which they would sit and listen to stories about pioneer days, Indian lore, patriotism and character, as well as jokes from instructors.

Because many of the boys had never seen a sunrise, never heard a coyote howl, never heard a whip-poor-will birdsong, or greeted the rising moon, this outing provided an experience that they would never forget.

Eight miles away was Lake Wallenpaupack, the third largest lake in Pennsylvania with a shoreline of fifty-two miles. Each summer, select campers hiked to this lake to camp on property owned by one of Beard's friends. Camp gear and supplies were taken to the site by trek carts (a wagon usually pulled by two or four campers, or by automobile.

CACHES

Overnight wilderness excursions need to *cache* - that is to hide or secure goods or provisions. Security of these *caches* is considered a must while wilderness camping because if the *cache* is not secured the provisions will be raided by bears, foxes, coyotes, porcupines, and racoons.

ILLUSTRATIONS BY Dan Beard from his book: Shelters, Shacks and Shanties, published in 1914, page 178.

Horsemanship and Marksmanship

Classes in horsemanship and marksmanship were added to the Outdoor School's activity program during the mid-1920's. Bartlett Beard learned riding skills and marksmanship skills while attending New York Military Academy, and was the primary instructor at the camp.

During the summer, up to a dozen horses were brought to the camp's stables by train from the Military Academy. Classes in horsemanship were extremely popular as many boys had no experience with such a large animal. While trail rides were the most common, the boys were also taught to ride at various gaits and over all kinds of terrain. They were also educated on caring for the horses and the riding gear. Inexperienced riders were taught to ride in the corral. Horsemanship skills included: tack-up (saddle and bridle the horse), tack-down (unsaddle and unbridle the horse); packing a horse for long-distance travel, cooling down after a ride, unraveling a

129

tangled tail or mane using a hard brush, soft brushing the rest of the horse's body, picking up and cleaning the horse's hoofs with a pick, and bathing the horse.

Marksmanship was another popular activity at the Outdoor School. Beard embraced the belief that shooting sports taught life-skills including discipline, responsibility, self-control, rewards of hard work, and respect for others. Not surprising, the Outdoor School had an outstanding safety record.

All shooting was performed at the shooting range under careful instructor supervision, and the boys learned to master safe gun handling and marksmanship skills. A small group of boys ages ten to twelve learned to shoot with Daisy 11 BB guns, and older boys used a single shot 22-caliber rifle. Winchester, Remington, and Savage rifles were popular, and several instructors and counselors brought their own guns. Targets were affixed to plywood boards and placed at various distances in front of a dirt berm. Campers learned to shoot from the standing, sitting, kneeling, and prone (lying on the ground) positions. Dan Beard stated many times:

> "It takes more than a boy, a rifle, and a box of ammunition to make a marksman. It takes practice and, by using proper methods, develops instinctively a coordination of keen eyes and steady nerves."

Rifle Range
RIFLE MARKSMANSHIP

Courtesy of Bartlett Beard

Good Horsemanship is having feel, timing and balance.
We must be able to control ourselves before we can
think we may be qualified to control the horse or a rifle.

Dan Beard

Courtesy of Bartlett Beard

LIGHTING THE COUNCIL FIRE
While our woodcrafter ignites the fire with rubbing sticks, the guardians of the four mystic fires of the East, North, West and South and a number of Indian dancers look on. The Medicine Man (seated in the background) beats a faster and faster rhythm on the Tom Tom, swelling to a climax as the cedar bark tinder bursts into flame.

Courtesy of Daniel Carter Wing Scrapbook Collection

THE MEDICINE MAN
Camp promotional pamphlet, 1922.

An invaluable step in character training is
to put responsibility on the individual.
Lord Baden-Powell

ON AN OVERNIGHT HIKE
Camp promotional pamphlet, 1922.

Merit Badges

B ecause the Boy Scout manual was used as the camp textbook for learning woodcraft and handicraft skills for all campers, Boy Scouts and campers who became Boy Scouts could earn merit badges. The most popular merit badges issued by the camp's Court of Honor were: Athletics, Aviation, Bugling, Camping, Conservation, First Aid, Handicrafts, Horseman-

L ike at Culver, each summer the camp was converted to a Boy Scout Troop.

The Dan Beard Camp was the Pike County, Pennsylvania, Troop #1 of the Boy Scouts of America. Boys ten and older could join the Troop and earn the required merit badges for the three classes of ranks: Tenderfoot, Second-Class Scout, and First-Class Scout. The boys could then transfer the badges they earned back to their home troop.

---

11 Daisy air rifles date back to 1888, when the company produced its first model. In those days, shot tubes were sized to utilize lead drop shot that was approximately .180 inches in diameter; a size referred to as "BB," thus the name "BB gun" still used today.

ship and Marksmanship (both
of which were introduced in
the late 1920's), Swimming and
Life-saving. Other merit badges
the boys could earn were
Angling, Cooking, First Aid,

> The Aviation merit badge began in 1911. Career opportunities in aviation were discussed as well as general airplane operations. When taught by a qualified instructor, an Aviation Merit Badge could be earned by a Boy Scout.

Forestry, Pathfinding, Personal Health, Pioneering, Signaling, Stalking (Tracking). According to the Boy Scouts of America, Dan Beard Council:

> *"It was the aim of the faculty to make the boys thorough in their work rather than to make a record of the numbers who won scouting degrees and honors, that is, we tried to make a merit badge and/or honors won at the Dan Beard Outdoor School, one which will be respected through scoutdom (sic) as an honor gained by hard work and thoroughness, and we are proud to report five boys passed the Tenderfoot test, and that seven were promoted to Second-Class Scouts, and three were promoted to First Class Scouts, and that there were 50 merit badges given by the Court of Honor during the eight-week season."*

In the late 1920s, boys who joined the camp's Lindbergh Club could make model airplanes and earn their Aviation Merit Badge.

Academic Instruction

Occasionally, there were requests from parents for their sons to have special instruction at the camp. The boys could receive academic instruction in the following subjects: arithmetic, elementary algebra, English grammar, English composition, public speaking, writing, mental arithmetic, and spelling. These subjects, taught by faculty, were upon request and without extra charge. During the first five years, a study tent was built for small group instruction and for campers to have a quiet environment for personal study sessions. In the 1919 camp brochure, Beard explained the opportunity for study sessions:

> *"This affords an opportunity for boys to engage in any study in which they may feel deficient. We think that something more serious than a simple, profitless vacation is due our boys and they are entitled to systemic instruction during the summer months. At our school we mingle recreation with education in such a manner that it's difficult to tell the beginning of one and the ending of the other."*

Games and Activities of Skill

Long before the advent of television and video games, games and activities requiring dexterity, strategy, and skill were popular as both a pastime and a competitive sport. One of the activities that Beard enjoyed instructing was the use of the tomahawk (or hatchet). Besides teaching them safe handling and cutting techniques, he taught them how to throw and strike the tomahawk into a "war post." Beard introduced tomahawk-throwing competitions at Culver and carried the activity over to his Outdoor School. The boys enjoyed it, and although it was somewhat dangerous, no accidents were ever reported.

In his 1909 book, *The Boy Pioneers, Sons of Daniel Boone,* Beard wrote about tomahawk throwing:

UNIQUE CEREMONY AT DAN BEARD CAMP
HAWLEY, PA.

"It was the ambition of the boys to be able to throw a toma-hawk with the skill and accuracy of our pioneer forebears, and the ability soon acquired by the boys in throwing hatchets at targets was really remarkable."

Tomahawk-throwing occurred almost every evening and became the highlight of the gatherings. All campers, instructors, and counselors participated in the activity of throwing the toma-hawk and competition was fierce among the stockades.

When Beard was well into his eighties he still remained a skillful thrower - a primary feature of his physical robustness. He explained:

"When I was a boy, I discovered by experiment that five steps, not paces was the right distance for which to throw the Tomahawk. The Tomahawk will make a given "x" number of turns in a given distance. In five steps it will make one turn and strike with the edge. Furthermore,

ten steps, fifteen steps, and even twenty steps is the right space when practice and muscle allow you to throw it that far."

Practice, practice, and more practice was necessary for campers to become good at tomahawk throwing. Each boy had to learn near-perfect coordination between mind and body in order to make a notable throw.

It was highly recommended that each camper have their own belt axe and pocket knife. The camp policy concerning the belt axe was that no camper would unsheathe his axe except when it was necessary to use for legitimate camp purposes, and no camper was

Despite the popular belief that tomahawks were used primarily in battle, Native American Indians would often throw them for fun. Tribes would hold contests and would also visit frontiersman's camps to compete with them. The word "tomahawk," comes from a transliteration of the Algonquin word meaning "strike down." The tomahawk is believed to have originated with the Iroquoian and Algonquian Indians, who also used them as tools, weapons, and as ceremonial pieces.

A war post is an old log or dead tree, the best being chestnut, which was set up at or near the council ground at the camp for the purpose of practice in throwing the tomahawk. The war post originated with the Mohawk Indians (of the Iroquois Confederacy). After a ceremonial dance, each man would come forward and strike his tomahawk into the post and recount his victories on the warpath.

allowed to throw the tomahawk at a living thing–be it a tree, plant, animal, or person..

Pocket knife games were also a popular pastime as well as extra entertainment for the campers. "Mumblety-peg" was a game in which the players attempted to flip a knife from various hand and body positions, sinking its blade into the ground. Two or more players would sit in a wide circle and each player would have his pocket knife's large blade opened. The game's objective was to perform all types of knife-throwing tricks where the knife's blade would stick into the ground. If the knife was angled in the ground, the handle could not be less than two finger widths above the earth. If a camper's throw did not land securely into the ground, the next thrower would take his turn.

The most popular series of knife throws for the peg game included:

1. Starting with the knife's blade lying point first between the thumb and first finger of the right hand, and flipping it into the ground, and then performing the same throw with the left hand.

2. Flinging the knife off the back of the hand.

3. Throwing the knife off the wrist.

4. Throwing the knife off the elbow.

5. Throwing the knife off the shoulder.

6. Bringing the handle up to the nose and flipping it over in the air.

7. Bringing the handle up to the right eye and flipping it over in the air, then repeating by first bringing it up to the left eye.

8. Flinging the knife off the head.

The higher up the body, the harder the throw needed to be. Campers completing the chosen knife throws were the winners and usually had an extra series of knife throws to decide the final winner. Campers typically played for a small prize such as a shooter marble. Unlike the game that originated in the British

Isles during the 17th century, losers were not required to pull or "mumble the peg" out of the ground with their teeth.

In a letter to parents about camp activities, Beard wrote about open recreation time each day. Playing (or "shooting" marbles was mentioned, and he suggested that boys interested in marble games should bring along their bag of marbles.

Shooting a marble was to "knuckle-down" in the dirt, pitching the marble in the bend of the index finger and then flicking it with the thumb. Shooters were required to keep

Glass marbles only began to be mass produced in 1915, but "shooting marbles" was first played centuries ago when pebbles were used instead, and the pebbles won were only valued as trophies or counters.

In marble shooting, a marble won is a point won in the game, and it is not necessary to keep the marbles after the game is over, any more than it is necessary to keep the balls and bats of the defeated baseball players or the football of the defeated football players. What the Outdoor School camper played for was to win the game, not the implements of the sport.

Shooter marbles (called Boss) were slightly larger and much fancier than regular marbles. Some marbles were made of steel and commonly called a steely. Steely marbles made the best shooter marbles.

at least one knuckle on the ground during the shot. Most of the shooting was done by rolling the shooter marble on the ground to hit a marble in the circle.

"Plunking" was the name of the shooting technique which involved shooting the marble high and hitting the targeted marble without hitting the ground. Playing "for keeps" meant that all campers' marbles knocked out of the ring could be kept as part of the shooter's personal collection.

So popular was this game that The Outdoor School constructed two flat dirt areas for marble shooting. A circle made in the dirt was called the boundary, or taw line, which was approximately ten feet in diameter. Each player placed marbles in the center of the ring for a total of thirteen, arranging them in an "X" formation called a "duck." Shooters then took turns knuckling down with their shooter marble and firing into the marbles to scatter them in the center of the ring. Any marbles leaving the ring belonged to the shooter. If a camper's shooter stayed in the ring after hitting a marble out over the taw line, he received another shot and continued until his shooter marble left the ring. Once all thirteen marbles had been knocked out of the ring, the game was over and a new set of marbles were re-racked into a "duck" for the next round. Campers who lost all their marbles had to trade or buy back marbles from the winners. Trading marbles was both a fun and anticipated activity at the Outdoor School.

RECESS HOUR

THE WINNING STOCKADE

"Expect a great deal of your boys
and you will generally get it."

—Bartlett Beard (1930)

PERSONAL INSPECTIONS

Camp promotional pamphlet, 1922
Courtesy of Bartlett Beard

A TYPICAL DAY AT THE OUTDOOR SCHOOL

he Outdoor School was the only non-military school that followed military-like discipline and conducted stringent personal and living-quarters inspections. The objectives of the school, derived from progressive[12] education principles, focused on the physical training, handicraft, and wood-craft activities taught at the school.

Beard described these objectives in the camp brochures:

" . . . To build the boys up physically, mentally, and spiritu-
ally and on this establish a foundation for abiding belief
in honor, sportsmanship, truthfulness, America and the
Creator; also to ground the boys in essentials of right

---

12 In 1910, there began a broadening in the recognition of the value of a pro-gressive education. Progressives believed that, if taught to understand the rela-tionship between thinking and doing, children would be fully equipped for active participation in a democratic society.

living; to train them to be leaders, that this generation of boys may be better American citizens in every respect to the one preceding it. The Dan Beard Outdoor School does not rely on precedents; it is here to establish them. It holds sacred only those things of yesterday which tend to promote advancement in morals, culture and physical strength, for tomorrow . . . "

For the first few years there was no bugler in camp to sound reveille and the boys were awakened about 5:30 a.m. by Beard coming down the trail from his cabin singing:

"Oh – ain't dis a mighty pretty morning
Good Lord – Good Lord
Oh – ain't dis a mighty pretty morning
Good Lord – Good Lord
De devil's mad and I am glad
Good Lord – Good Lord
He lost a soul - he thought he had
Good Lord – Good Lord . . ."

Once all the boys were dressed in their swimming suits and in formation in front of their tents, a series of stretching exercises using a towel for resistance was lead by the stockade leaders. These stretches, which were meant to get the circulation moving, were followed by the morning "plunge" in the lake.

After the morning bath/swim, the boys assembled near the Council grounds for ten minutes of more vigorous exercise. These exercises, called "setting-up exercises" followed the same format and routine used by the military: four-count push-ups, sit-ups, side-straddle hops (jumping-jacks), burpees (a squat thrust

"Setting-Up Exercises" was a term first used in the early 1900s, and which is defined as "any of a series of gymnastic exercises used to give a boy good posture, build muscle tone, easy control of the limbs (flexibility) and weight loss through calorie burn." Popular exercises done at the Outdoor School included push-ups, sit-ups, side-straddle hop (jumping jacks), trunk twisters and knee bends.

beginning and ending in the standing position), alternate toe touches, and trunk twisters.

Beaumert Whitton, a camper and Boy Scout, explained one unique exercise designed by Beard called the "eye drill":

"This drill will improve your eyesight and help to correct any tendency toward incomplete focusing of the eyes. You must remember that the eye is a round ball held in place by four muscles; if one of these muscles is a little stronger than the others, it pulls the eye in its direction and throws it out of focus; therefore, if we exercise these muscles systematically, we are bound to give more or less equal strength to all four muscles."

Following the exercises, the boys dressed in their uniforms, cleaned their tents (which were inspected daily), and lined up in stockade formation preparing to march to breakfast. Following breakfast at 7:00 a.m., three hours were devoted to instruction in various school activities. Then came the regular morning swim at 11:00 a.m. Beginner swimmers were taught during this time frame, and advanced swimmers worked on distance swimming and diving.

For an hour after lunch there was a rest period devoted to receiving daily mail, writing letters, and general visitation with other campers. Beard required that a boy write to his parents or guardian at least once a week.

145

From 2:00 to 4:00 p.m., campers participated in organized athletic events or special activities such as horsemanship and marksmanship, or were provided instruction on activities such as log-cabin building. At 4:00 p.m., an afternoon free swim was scheduled and usually continued until time for the boys to dress for dinner which was promptly served at 6:00 p.m. Following dinner, there were games, boating, tomahawk-throwing contests, lasso-throwing contests, and story-telling (usually by special guests visiting Beard) except on Saturdays when the Council Fires were the highlight of the evening. At 8:30 p.m., the boys began to prepare for *Taps* at 9:00 p.m. before turning in for the night.

Saturdays and Sundays

Weekends at camp were a joyful time for the boys; parents would visit[13], and there were many guests. Although Saturdays were as busy as any other day-with regular classes and training-the evenings were pure fun and excitement. Festivities began at the evening meal when, as soon as the tables were cleared, the campers would sing "heart songs," which only heightened the enthusiasm and fervor for the evening's events. At dusk, which was around 9 p.m., the Council Fire ceremonies would begin and would last about an hour or two.

Sundays were a day of fun and relaxation. The day would begin a half-an-hour later than the rest of the week, with reveille at 6:30 a.m. The boys would do their morning plunge in the lake, exercises, inspections, and march to the mess hall for an 8 a.m.

---

13 Visiting parents and guests from out of town were invited to stay at Beard's lodge, "Wildlands" at no charge.

"Heart Songs" were well-known American folk songs, many of which are still sung today. Among the favorites sung by the boys after Saturday evening meals were "Take Me Out to the Ball Game," "Old MacDonald Had a Farm," and "If You're Happy and You Know It." A part of government-funded programs to put people to work during the Great Depression, the Roosevelt administration's Works Progress Administration (WPA) created programs to document traditions of rural peoples through writing or sound recordings. Scholars worked to document both stories and songs by writing them down or by using recording equipment if available.

breakfast. Sundays were also a day for the boys to look their best and wear their formal uniforms.

Instead of classes or hikes, everyone–to include visiting parents and guests–would attend religious services beginning at 10 a.m. Services were non-denominational and held at the "outdoor cathedral," which was a clearing in the woods near the main road where wooden chairs were set up (On rainy days, services were held in the mess hall or camp headquarters.) Each week a minister from a different religious denomination would lead the service.

Following the service, lunch was served at noon, and from 1:30 to 4:30 the boys spent time with their parents, showing them the handicrafts they made and demonstrating their favorite activities-which almost always included tomahawk throwing!

For those boys whose parents were not visiting that week, it was open recreation time. They went swimming and horseback riding, played games of marbles and mumblety-peg, and whittled and worked on handicrafts. Socializing between the stockades was widely encouraged.

Around 4:30, parents would say their farewells to their sons knowing that their boys were in good hands and were enjoying the opportunity of a lifetime at the Dan Beard Camp. The boys would march to dinner at 5 p.m. and enjoy an evening of games and socializing before *Taps* was played at 9 p.m.

With drums and bugles, marching from mess full of wholesome food and wholesome thoughts

THE MESS HALL

A screened pavilion proudly decorated with the totems of the winning stockades
Courtesy of Bartlett Beard

CEREMONIES AND AWARDS

Camp ceremonies were designed to celebrate the sense of community and camaraderie at the camp as well as the accomplishments of the boys. Acknowledging and rewarding their determination and commitment not only boosted morale and made the boys feel valued, but also motivated the others by setting an example for them to aspire to.

Council Fires

Beard initiated Council Fires at the Culver Woodcraft School, and carried over the tradition to his Outdoor School. A special 'council grounds' area had been set aside when the camp was being built, specifically for these gatherings. The Council Fires, which were held every Saturday evening, were ceremonies filled with mystery, excitement, and pageantry- and the most highly anticipated event of the week!

The main purpose for these Council Fires was for the boys to receive awards and demonstrate skills they had learned-and occasionally, a tomahawk throwing contest was held. Buckskin costumes from Beard's personal collection were worn by the instructors to bring to life the days of the early pioneers.

The Indian invocation, the fire-lighting ceremony, and the pinning of awards, all had a magical aura. The "Chief," dressed in his white buckskin outfit, pinned the awards won by each boy onto their uniforms.

In an article for *Boys' Life*, Bertram Broome chronicled the ebullience of the Council Fire ceremonies:

> *"Shortly after sunset a bugle sounds the 'assembly' and before its sweet tones have faded to an echo all the boys of the D.B.O.S. and the instructors assemble at the Council Grounds and stand in half-moon formation facing a rustic pulpit draped with skins of wolf, fox, wildcat and deer. Back of the pulpit hangs a large moose skin, part of a trophy brought out of the Canadian woods by Mr. Beard, whose power as a hunter is as famous as his other attainments.*
>
> *On the four sides of the Council Grounds and about seventy-five feet apart, stand four rustic fire-towers upon whose elevated floors of earth and clay are the fire sticks and timber ready to ignite . . . The tower-fires now blaze up brightly, fed by a boy at each tower.*
>
> *Now comes the award of honors and merit badges won by the boys individually and as 'stockades' (troops) for swimming, hiking canoeing, tests, and most coveted of all, inspection, the daily evening full dress inspection that*

precedes 'to the color' ceremony and in which each boy competes with the keenness of a West Point Cadet. After the awards are made, invited guests address the boys on various subjects and visiting fathers voice their views and appreciation of the school and its wonderful work. The ceremonies close with real Indian chants, and a final speech and invocation by Chief Beard.

The entire school, visiting parents, guests from the Forest Lake Club, neighbors from cottages across the lake, friends of the Beard family, and girls from nearby Camp Douglas, all enjoyed the splendor of the Council Fires. This was one of the few times girls were invited to the camp. Alice Finney, whose mother was director of Camp Douglas, recounted the reactions of the girls:

"One of the big events of the week was the Council Fire and our whole camp always attended. It would usually be about dusk when we all got settled down and then the four watch tower fires (on the points of the compass) would be lit one-by-one on call. On the call each fire would leap up (something I have never made a wood fire do!) and they used to say each fire had a little bit of Dan Beard magic on it.

Uncle Dan was really a true woodsman, an ardent conservationist, an expert axe thrower (even when he was quite old) and a marvelous showman. When he used to step out in his gleaming, white smoke cured fringed buckskin shirt and pants-lighted only with the firelight-and with all the boys seated around the totem poles, etc.-all the girls were practically swimming with excitement and romance."

It was the opinion of the boys, guests, and parents alike that Dan Beard was offering something very special and worthwhile at the Outdoor School.

Honor Awards

In all competitive activities at the camp, such as inspection of tents, inspection of each individual, and in competitive games, the winning stockade was awarded by a red, white, and blue streamer (ribbon with a brass sleigh-bell at one end. The ribbon was fastened to the winning stockade's totem pole. The poorest performing stockade received a "chump" mark, which was a yellow ribbon fastened to their totem pole. Competition among stockades included: inspection of tents, personal inspection which included uniform inspections, posture, honors for "deeds of conspicuous merit," best behavior, competitive games and cleanliness of hands, fingernails, and teeth. At the conclusion of the eight-week session, the totem poles presented a striking appearance.

Each year the winning stockade's totem was permanently placed on the roof of the mess hall and the other poles were displayed around the camp grounds. The idea behind doing this was to foster a healthy spirit of rivalry and espirit-de-corps.

When boys achieved individual merits, they received a red, white and blue ribbon, called a "nick," which was worn just above their heart. Ten nicks made a notch, which was an honor mark worn on the left sleeve of the uniform. Besides merit notches, special notches were awarded for expertise in forestry, fire-building, pioneering, plant knowledge, handicraft, bird knowledge and similar feats. Special notches were called "top-notch" awards. A handicraft top-notch was awarded for the crafting of outstanding items including the neckerchief slide, leather tabs, knife sheath, a fire-making set, ditty bag, Belmore Brown pack strap, bow and arrows; quiver (a basket used to hold the bow and arrows), beaded work in the form of a ring or hat band, and chip flint arrow-head.

Campers had to win the required number of notches before they were eligible for the bronze medal of the Cub Bears, the silver medal of the Black Bears, or the gold medal of the Grizzly Bears. The boys strove to have the left arm of their uniform decorated from shoulder to cuff with the brilliant insignia representing notches. In their effort to win distinction, they learned to be industrious, studious, and cooperative. Some boys elected to wear their awards on their dress hat.

Named for Belmore Brown (1880-1954), a hunter, artist, photographer, and writer, the 'Belmore Brown pack strap' was designed with a padded yoke that fit across the breastbone and over the shoulders of the wearer, with the ends of the yoke connecting to the pack. The weight was exerted downward, enabling better carriage and less fatigue.

As an Alaskan explorer and consultant and lecturer on arctic survival, Browne was considered an expert on cold weather survival techniques. He is most famous for his 1913 conquest of Mt. McKinley in Alaska.

Like the medals the boys earned for swimming achievements, bronze, silver and gold medals for high honors were awarded to individuals as well. Each represented accomplishments in progressively difficult skills. Additional honor awards included: Best All-Around Woodcrafter, Woodcrafter Showing Most Improvement, Woodcrafter receiving the most honor ribbons, Junior Wood-crafter receiving the most ribbons, Best Leatherworkers in Camp, Leading Student of Aviation, Best Horsemanship Student, Scout Earning the Most Merit Badges, and Winning Stockade.

Honor Fraternities

Prior to 1918, boys aged ten to eighteen could become Buckskin Men. Campers were chosen to become Buckskin Men based on their character and tenacity. Howard Hughes, a camper in 1916 who was only ten at the time, and Beard's ten-year-old son, Bartlett, in 1917, along with twenty-three other campers, counselors, and instructors were initiated into the Buckskin Fraternity.

The fraternity was formed for two primary reasons. First, boys would come back to camp year after year in an attempt to become a Buckskin Man because the instructors, along with Beard, needed more time to evaluate campers. Second, a boy of fifteen years selected for his standards of character and integrity of American institutions could become a member of the Buckskin Men. Buckskin Men had their own lodge (a tepee) built for them by Hudson Bay Indians. The lodge was not used for housing but rather only by members for meetings, fraternity business, and socializing. This novel fraternity bound themselves by a pledge, oath, and promise. Each boy wore a badge of Buckskin on which was branded the powder horn of Danial Boone. This badge was the most highly prized decoration among the older campers.

1917 Outdoor School promotional catalog.

154

The Buckskin oath, pledge and promise were given to the recipient at a Saturday evening Council Fire ceremony. Beard stressed that the objective of this society was "character building and the preservation of the vigor and integrity of American institutions." A Scout executive would initiate the Buckskin Men with an ancient Indian initiation, which was spectacular but secret in nature. During the ceremony, Beard gave each of the Buckskin Men a thin slice of smoked Grizzly Bear jerky meat and a whiff of musky, vanilla-scented Beaver castor. As they ate the jerky, Beard told them that, " ... this will give the body and soul strength and courage from this great animal." Also, by inhaling the odor from the medicine flask that was given to Beard by Bow-Arrow, the Chief of the Montagnais Indians, "one's body and soul will have a great and abiding love of the outdoors.'"

In the summer of 1918, Beard formed the Leather Stocking Boys, a fraternity for the younger campers ages ten to fourteen. It was the goal of boys under age fifteen to become a Leather Stocking. As part of the Buckskin Men ceremony, the Leather Stocking Boys repeated the Leather Stocking law and oath at the Council Fire just before the Buckskin Men were honored.

Beard, when awarding the Leather Stocking badges proclaimed:

"You are treading in the footsteps of the Buckskin Men. You will soon wear the complete Buckskin costume and do all that the full-fledged Buckskin Men do. Be strong and valiant as the Frontier men, who tramped through the wilderness and crossed the plains, the men who build our grand empire, America, and left those inspiring names for our

'Hall of Fame'-Daniel Boone, Davy Crockett, Simon Kenton, Lewis and Clark and hosts of others still following the greatest pioneer of all who spurs us on to higher and greater deeds of valor and accomplishment. I congratulate you."

When people started talking about "The Hunger Games" I realized I could survive longer than most of my friends because of the skills I learned at camp.

Camp Confessions (LCMC)

THE WINTER CAMP

F or one week following Christmas, boys had the opportunity to return to the Outdoor School for winter camp. Each parent received a letter similar to the summer camp letter, but the winter camp letter detailed what type of clothing to bring for camping and hiking in the snow. The winter "uniform" included a cap of woolen felt that could be pulled down over the ears, a Mackinaw wool coat (called a "Mack"), a pair of wool pants[13] leggings (heavy woolsocks), boot packs (rubber shoes with an oiled leather boot legs laced up the front-similar to what is known today as "duck boots"), mittens and wool gloves (to wear inside of the mittens), and camouflage[14]-like

---

13 Wool pants - If parents made the boys' winter pants or other clothing, it was recommended that they use wool fabric or heavy wool blanket material.
14 Camouflage - The boys were encouraged to bring clothing in "woodsy" colors that would camouflage" them when they hiked in the snowy woods. Camouflage clothing, worn by hunters today, was not invented or manufactured until 1986.

clothing (to be worn over their regular clothes) for hiking and watching wildlife.

The cost of the camp, over the years, ranged from $20.00 to $30.00. Because the boys had to give up their short school holiday vacation to attend the camp, the winter camp was not as popular as the summer Outdoor School. In addition, because of staffing problems, financial concerns, and the demand for Beard's time among his other commitments, the

Drawing by Dan Beard.
Clemens and Sibley's Book: <u>Uncle Dan</u>, p.211

winter camp was not held every winter, and camp attendance was usually ten boys or less.

During the winter camp, both boys and instructors lived in Beard's log home. A large fireplace and an old-fashioned coal stove heated the cabin, and the home served as an open dormitory, meeting room, and ideal setting for story-telling. Mrs. Beard, along with a local woman who assisted her, provided the meals for the campers, and Beard's son, Bartlett, served as an instructor. Activities consisted of ice skating and skate sailing, hockey, ice boating, snowshoeing, cross country skiing, and hiking.

When the temperature was expected to be over twenty degrees, overnight hikes were planned using equipment from the Outdoor School. Beard had a winter overnight campsite constructed not far from his log cabin. The site was surrounded by large boulders to reflect the heat from the camp fire, which that was built with small logs or heavy bark on trampled-down snow. It was designed to burn all night to provide heat for the tents. Dinner and breakfast were prepared over the fire by older campers under the supervision of instructors.

Most of the hiking was done during the day, and a typical day hike had an early morning departure and explored the trails surrounding the camp.

> "A hiking expedition may set off in the morning and explore the trails leading into the woods or frozen swamps [that were] inaccessible in summer. At noon, they stop at some dry sheltered ledge and build a fire, heat some cocoa, broil their meat, and ration out the grub brought from camp. They return in the afternoon for a big dinner, the comfort of an open fireplace and talk about the hike."

Basic survival skills were taught inside the warm cabin to all winter campers after the evening meal. The winter camp instructors' goals were to prepare boys to survive in the wilderness using nature's resources. While most boys immediately focused on finding food, they were taught that food rated low on the list of survival priorities. They learned that shelter, water (especially in cold climates), and fire were the most urgent needs. Tips for building a wilderness shelter were discussed and all boys participated in constructing a shelter using natural materials with instructors' guidance and assistance. (Think of how rewarded a boy would feel to have built a fire without matches, gathered and prepared edible plants and insects for food, and to have stocked and hunted with their own handmade bow and arrow, or trapped small game for food.) Other survival skills learned at winter camp were knot-tying, first aid basics, making rope from natural materials, cold weather first aid, and ice rescue.

Illustrated by Dan Beard from his book THE OUTDOOR HANDY BOOK,
Charles Scribner's Sons, 1904, p. 452

THE LEGACY OF
DAN BEARD

Our values guide us and help us to achieve the life we want to live while contributing to the world- and to the future. Leaving a legacy develops from dedication and purpose. It's not about remembering someone's name, but rather who they were.

Dan Beard started the Outdoor School based on his belief that no institute of learning taught the little things, the timely things, and the historically "American" things that all boys should know. None of them emphasized the mental and physical importance of sport, without the requirement to spend a lot of money on equipment. Beard encouraged the sports that pioneer boys may have played out in the wilderness.

During the latter years (1930's), the "Chief" was not involved in the day-to-day activities of the camp because that responsibility had been passed on to his son. However, as the main attraction, he continued to make appearances in his buckskin outfits, sat with the boys and told stories of the "good old days," and gave inspirational talks at the Council Fires.

Simple living modeled after that of the American pioneers and made more appealing to the modern boy by use of colorful Native American symbolism, a commitment to Boy Scout virtues, and promoting a sense of pride in American citizenship and values made the Outdoor School different from other boys' camps. Beard's ceremonies, sensational pageants, nature study, and handicraft and woodcraft activities, provided a real and vital purpose in the physical, psychological, and moral development of the boys who attended his camps, which better prepared them to become genuine "leaders" of the future.

During the 1920's, the Outdoor School was at its peak both financially and in enrollments. Although Beard was well into his seventies, the emphasis remained on outdoor activities as opposed to athletics. The philosophy of the school did not change, with Beard routinely reminding his staff that "a boy should be taught independence and be given the opportunity to care for himself." An environment of high moral integrity was exemplified by the staff and demanded of the campers. His influence in creating interest in the outdoors over three generations was legendary.

Above all, Dan Beard was an American, steeped in American tradition and passing on the torch of American democracy to the future through his boys.

The Dan Beard Outdoor School closed in 1938 when Beard was eighty-eight years of age. He died on June 12, 1941-just ten days shy of his ninety-first birthday. The Dan Beard Camp,

Inc., sat on approximately twenty-seven wooded acres on the edge of Lake Teedyuskung, near Hawley, Pennsylvania. In 1943, parcels of the land were sold off by the Beard estate, with Bartlett Beard acting as executor.

The only log cabin from Beard's camp that exists today is the one built in 1926 called "Camp Headquarters." This large twenty-eight by thirty foot cabin, with a wrap-around porch and stone fireplace, was primarily used as a large assembly room. It also housed several staff and instructors in four upstairs bedrooms.

In 2011, Woodloch Pines Resort, which now sits on the site of the Dan Beard Outdoor School for Boys, donated this historic cabin to the Boy Scouts of America. The Northeast Pennsylvania (NEPA) Counsel of the Boy Scouts of America moved the cabin to the Goose Pond Boy Scout Reservation about fifteen miles from Hawley, Pennsylvania.

There is no evidence that writings are a complete history of Dan Beard's Woodcraft Camps. Persons with additional information not found in this book are invited to forward new information to wmkahler@gmail.com for possible inclusion in a later edition.

TREASURES
FROM THE
ARCHIVES

Dan Beard Writes about the Summer Woodcraft Camp at Culver

With the National Scout Commissioner

WOODCRAFT CAMP—CULVER ACADEMY

BY DANIEL CARTER BEARD

FELLOW SCOUTS: I am writing this in the camp, where I have about forty as fine Scouts as you ever saw. We have just finished our lessons in throwing the diamond hitch, the lariat and fire building. All of the Scouts have passed the test of building fire with one match. Many of them built the fire in pouring rain, using only the wet wood that they found in the woods, and all of them have built it when the wind was blowing briskly. They have also passed the test of naming and describing the required number of plants and forest trees, as well as the birds and fishes. We have a number of plants and forest trees. We have a permit from the game warden to use a seine in Lake Maxinkuckee, and by this means we are able to secure specimens of all the varieties of fish inhabiting these waters. Some of these we preserve for our museum; most of them we release; but the smaller ones we save for a fine, big aquarium made under my directions for the camp. I only wish that all the Scouts could be as happily situated as are my chosen forty. My! my! my! You should see them in the water drawing that seine! If the fishes had ears there wouldn't be one on our side of the lake, because the boys yell like a band of Apache Indians.

Last night we had a hike out to a neighboring wood, where we cooked our supper and had a council fire. Each one of the officers sang a song or told a story; but one of us did both. Our order of business was for the troops or stockades to form in a double line in front of the camp, then march up to the council fire, the line dividing and those on the right marching in that direction, while those on the left took the opposite direction until they formed a semi-circle around the council fire. Each of the Scouts held a blazing torch in his hand of his own manufacture, made after the description and diagrams given in the Field and Forest Handbook. At the command, "Squat!" they seated themselves cross-legged like a row of tailors, then at the word of command each of them arranged his firewood, after which their leader passed along the line, giving each Scout a single match. Again at the word of command the fires were lighted and the forty little blazes luminated the circle and cast a ruddy glare on forty tanned and happy faces.

During the camp fire meet the majority of the boys passed their flap-jack test, each of them cooking his own flap-jack and toastng it in the air, so that when it completed its somersault it alighted in the frying pan with the brown side up, and to prove that the flap-jacks themselves were a success they were all of them greedily devoured by the Scouts.

We sharpened and peeled the ends of the forks of green wands, impaled our bacon with the forks and cooked it over the glowing embers. We fried potatoes and made pots of steaming hot chocolate, neither tea or coffee being used in the Woodcraft Camp. Then each troop gave their own peculiar yell, keeping it up till pandemonium reigned, and the squirrels in the hollows crawled down to the deepest recesses to hide away from the din. After this merit-marks in the form of Notches and Nicks were awarded; then the trappings were gathered up, each troop forming in line with its respective leader, with the guides in the

front rank, the whole long column started Indian file through the dark woods down through a 'swail and a thicket, across a small stream, in the bright moonlight of the open-fields until they hit the home trail.

The boys have been rowing under their Chief and Ensign from the Naval Academy. They have swimming under a competent and experienced swimming master, and most of them have already passed their two hundred and fifty-yard test.

When the gun fires in the morning at five minutes of six o'clock the Scouts all tumble out of their berths and line up in the middle of the camp street, dressed in their bathing suits. Here they are put through a drill with their towels to warm them up. The last Scout out runs the gauntlet and is whipped in place with the towels of his fellow-Scouts. Then they trot down to the sandy beach of beautiful Lake Maxinmuckee and go splashing into the clear water. After a thorough ducking they come back on a trot, again line up and go through Muldoon's circulation exercise, first stooping and rubbing the right instep, then the left instep, then the right shin, then the left shin, using both hands with which to rub their limbs. Next they rub the calves of both legs, then they take the thumb and index fingers of each hand, put them on each side of the knee caps and rub them up and down. Next they briskly massage their thighs; then they knead their stomachs with their open hands, after which they beat a tattoo by slapping their chests with their open palms. Then the right arm is rubbed, next the left arm, after that both hands are used to rub the back of their necks, and the stunt is finished off by using the index fingers to rub up and down the temples.

After they are all well warmed up with this exercise they are ordered back to their tents for their tooth powder and tooth brushes; then they file out to where a spring bubbles up through an iron pipe, and here their teeth receive a thorough scouring. Each Scout, as he returns, holds up the wet tooth brush and grins to show that his teeth are clean. After this ceremony and fun is over all the bedding is taken out of the tents to be aired. You can imagine what a bustle there is when you know that the last troop to have its bedding out gets a chump mark, which stands against that particular troop, while the first troop gets a merit mark in the form of a Nick, which stands to the credit of that particular stockade. Now comes mess call, and the duties of the day have begun. So busy are we that night comes all too soon.

We are now busily engaged in carving out totem poles and painting them preparatory to erecting them in front of each troop, for next week we are to have a pageant on the water with torches and lanterns and all sorts of decorations, music and high jinks. I often wonder if the boys to-day really appreciate what a bully time they are having. It is a great thing to be a boy, but it is a much greater thing to be a Scout! Good luck and a good time to all of you.

Dan Beard

17

Handicrafts Created by Dan Beard

Dan Beard Tells You How

To Make a Noggin*

By DAN BEARD

National Scout Commissioner, Boy Scouts of America.

THE members of the Camp Fire Club of America, which, as you know, is composed of "boy" scouts anywhere from twenty-five to seventy-five years old, take great pride in their drinking cups which they carry at their belts. These cups cannot be purchased at a store. They are the result of true scout work, and hard work at that. It is against the traditions of the club for a member to wear a noggin made by himself. After he has made a beautiful cup he presents it to some other member. I have two of them—one made by the Vice-President of the club, Mr. George Hubbel, and presented to me, and one made by a whole bunch of the men, each one working upon it so that I should have the result of their united labor.

Every first class scout should carry one of these pioneer drinking cups.

Not only were the cups of our pioneer ancestors made of burls, but the porringers, from which they ate their cornmeal mush, and various other household utensils were also manufactured by hollowing out those warts, tumors or bunions which you see growing upon the trunks of trees.

Select a burl a little larger than the intended cup, because you must allow for the thickness of the bark. Take your jack-knife and cut off the outer rind from the highest point of the knob. Do this to see whether or not there is a hole in the burl, or a decayed spot, in which case discard it. You want a sound burl. (Fig. 1E.)

Now, saw off from the trunk of the tree, close to the tree, the lump or burl as in Fig. 2. To do this, it may be necessary to climb the tree and support yourself with a strap like a lineman (Fig. 1), though if you are lucky you may find one which you can reach by standing on the ground.

There must be a place for the handle where you fasten the thong, and this must be allowed for as that shown in A, Fig. 2. If you have a vise handy, hold your burl in the vise before you remove the bark, then bore a number of holes in the upper surface as shown by Fig. 3, after which, with elbow grease and perseverance, you carve out the inside.

When you have made a rough hollow, you may peel off the bark and then you must use great care not to make a hole through your cup, for many a good noggin is spoiled by carelessness in digging out the inside.

Almost any wood is good material for a noggin. Maple, cedar, spruce, white pine or birch can be worked into a beautiful one, while oak, although hard to cut, when finished gives probably the most serviceable one. I made one of wild cherry for Mr. George D. Pratt, President of the Camp Fire Club, and Treasurer of the Boy Scouts of America.

Many a cup of tea have I quaffed from a noggin in the far North, and many a delicious draught of cold spring water have I imbibed from a burl noggin in all parts of the wild country. The noggin is typically an American article and it is just the thing to busy yourself with this month. When you have the cup thin enough to

suit your fancy (but not thin enough to be easily cracked and broken) smooth it both inside and out with sandpaper—do not leave it half finished—then put it in a pail of linseed oil and leave it soak overnight, or for a day or two, after which polish it up by hand with the use of a flannel rag or a piece of buckskin. If you will take some beeswax and melt it, then pour some turpentine into the wax and stir it up until you make a thick paste then rub this paste thoroughly into the cup, you will get a surface that will take on a beautiful polish which nothing but hot water will destroy.

But!! Do not, under any consideration, bring your turpentine near the fire, or even in the room where there is a fire; take the melted beeswax away somewhere, where there are neither fire, candles or lamps burning, and then it will be safe; the beeswax will not set it afire.

In the handle of the cup bore a small hole, big enough for a "whang" string, that is, a thong (Fig. 4), such as you can buy at the country hardware shops and harness stores for about 10 cents. Slit the end of the whang string into three parts so as to make the knot shown in Fig. 5. Now take a stick of any kind of wood which is easy to whittle (Fig. 6), cut off a piece (Fig. 7) and carve it into the form shown by Fig. 8 to make the seymour. Bore a hole through the seymour, then run your whang string through the hole (Fig. 9) down to the knot which you have just tied; put the other end of the whang string through the hole in the handle of the noggin (Fig. 10) and knot the end so it cannot slip out.

Now, push the seymour up under your belt (Fig. 11) until it protrudes from above and your cup is ready for use at any moment, and if you push it around back of you it will be out of the way.

Tell your Scoutmasters to urge every First Class scout to produce a noggin of his own manufacture and that will set the boys going. Of course, some Second Class fellows may be clever and persistent enough to make a good noggin.

Go to it!

The fewer tools you have the more pride you can take in your cup.

16

How to Throw a Tomahawk

In the good old days when our brave pioneer ancestors carried long rifles with barrels made of imported horseshoe nails, the wooden stock trimmed with brass and ornamented with eagles, 'coons, deer, and other objects cut from shells and set into the wood, they also carried tomahawks. Trusty tomahawks in the leather belt which encircled the waist and belted in the wammus—and, like their neighbors, the redskins, many of the picturesque old fellows were expert in the use of these little camp axes as weapons of offence and defense.

Weapons of Pioneers

But the great Daniel Boone himself carried a small camp axe, almost the same as we use now, and the trees he blazed with this tomahawk to mark the boundaries of land were so well known as "Boone trees" that in after years lawsuits were decided by the identification of the blazed boundaries as the ones made by the stroke of Boone's tomahawk. This identical tomahawk of Boone's, along with one of Boone's traps, is now in the possession of a gentleman in Ohio.

When the writer was a small lad in Kentucky, it was the ambition of the boys, not to go and kill Indians, but to be able to throw a tomahawk with the skill and accuracy of our pioneer forebears, and the ability soon acquired by the boys in throwing hatchets at targets was really remarkable. They would come up to within thirty feet of an old board fence with a whoop and a yell, then "click! click! click!" would go the hatchets, each and every one sticking fast in the board, either in a true vertical or horizontal line as it pleased them. Ever since those glorious days of my boyhood in Kentucky it has seemed to me that throwing the tomahawk should be one of the regular feats at all American athletic meets.

Throwing the Tomahawk

For the benefit of the loyal scouts, I have made a series of sketches showing how to throw a hatchet, camp axe, or tomahawk, so that with a little practice the reader can astonish his friends with his skill in handling this truly American weapon. The practice is a splendid outdoor exercise, and one that trains the eyes and muscles even better than archery. Furthermore, the skill thus acquired may prove of signal service to any of the boys whose business or pleasure in after life takes them into wild and unexplored wilder-

by Dan Beard

nesses, for a well-thrown camp axe will split the skull of as large a monster as the grizzly bear.

When the youngsters first took up the tomahawk as a plaything, of course they were very awkward in its use. There was no one to show them, and no book like this to tell them how to do anything they wanted to do, so they had to learn from experiments.

It took a long time to find out how to hold the implement as shown in Fig. 233. Each lad, without exception, began by grasping the handle of the hatchet any old way, swung it in a curve, and let it go while the blade was in a diagonal or slanting position. This would send it wobbling through the air like a boomerang, with poor results as to marksmanship, and no power to stick into the mark, for, even when the blade by chance hit the mark, it struck across the grain and the axe fell to the ground. But at last we learned to stand firmly before the mark with our feet spread apart, the weight of the body resting upon the right leg, as in Figs. 233, 234, and 235.

Fig. 233
Correct Position for Throw

We also learned to take aim, not by sighting along the hatchet, but by fixing our eyes on the mark, and so holding our weapon that its edge formed part of the vertical line A B, Fig. 233.

When the tomahawk is brought back from position in Fig. 233, over the shoulder as in Figs. 234 and 235, without turning the edge to one side or the other, and thrown from this position, the blade cleaves its way straight through the air, and the air itself tends to keep it true to its course.

Figs. 234, 235
Keep the Blade in a Vertical Line

169

Fig. 236
Note How the Hatchet Strikes Its Edge Between Turns Shown by Dotted Line

How to Score a Hit

Take aim, as in Fig. 233, bring the tomahawk back over the shoulder, as in Figs. 234 and 235, then bring your hand quickly down, following the line A B, Fig. 233, and, swinging the body forward, let fly the tomahawk as in Fig. 236.

The weapon will turn over and over, as shown by the dotted line in the diagram. At a distance of about ten feet it will make two turns and stick (C, Fig. 236). Of course, you must learn to gauge the distance so that at the end of the last somersault the hatchet will strike the target with the cutting edge, as in Fig. 236, so that it will stick.

If the distance of the throw is to be increased, one must be sure to step back far enough to allow the hatchet to make another somersault and a rise before the cutting edge can bit. It is generally safe to count on a revolution and a half to make a hit, and one soon learns to gauge this distance, and can add or subtract a hitting distance by stepping forward or backward, as the case may be. Not only can this be done, but the novice will learn to measure a distance with his eyes, and, even at a long throw, will instinctively know whether to step forward or backward in order to make a hit, and he will also know just how his hatchet will strike the target.

Diagrams and talk can explain all this, but only practice can produce the skill and judgment which makes one so ready and rapid with the tomahawk that we call the action instinctive.

Team-Work in Tomahawking

After the boys in Kentucky had acquired some skill, our greatest fault in team-work lay, not in striking out of the line, but in so delivering our tomahawks as to split the handles of those already sticking in the target.

The prettiest feature of hatchet throwing is team-work, and after you have learned to send the tomahawk whirling through the air, each one quickly following the other, so that the last one strikes the target before the first ceases to quiver, all exactly in a vertical line (Fig. 237), then it is time to attempt the more difficult feat of sinking your hatchet in the target in a horizontal line (Fig. 238); but, after this is accomplished, any sort of fancy figure that you may desire may be made on the target with the tomahawks, the simplest of which is the cross (Fig. 239).

Figs. 237, 238
The Work of a Good Team

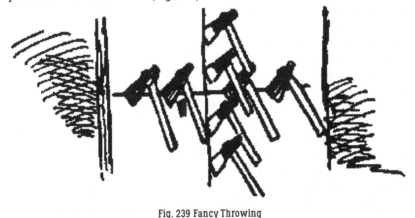

Fig. 239 Fancy Throwing

171

How to Play Mumbly Peg

ASummer's day, a shady nook, a close-cropped green sod, two or three boys, and a jack-knife are the things necessary for a quiet game of Mumbly Peg [or mumbley peg, mumblety peg, mumble peg, mumble-the-peg, mumbypeg, or mumble de peg].

The first player takes the knife and goes through as much of the game as he can without a blunder. The second follows in turn, doing the same. The last one to perform all of the difficult feats is beaten, and must pull a peg, two inches long, from the ground with his teeth. The winner drives the peg with the knife-handle for a hammer, being allowed, by the rules of the game, three blows with his eyes open, and three with his eyes closed.

This usually drives the peg out of sight in the sod, and in that case the boys cry:

"Root! Root!"

as the defeated player, using only his teeth, literally roots, until, with a dirty face and a broad grin, he lifts his head, showing the peg between his teeth. From the penalty that the loser pays comes the name of Mumbly or Mumbelty-Peg.

The Feats

<u>First</u>: Hold the right fist with back to the ground and with the jackknife, with blade pointing to the right, resting on top of the closed fingers (Fig. 282). The hand is swung to the right, up and over, describing a semicircle, so that the knife falls point downward and sticks, or should stick, upright in the ground (Fig. 283). If there is room to slip two fingers, one above the other, beneath the handle of the knife and if the point of the knife is hidden in the ground, it counts as a fair stick or throw.

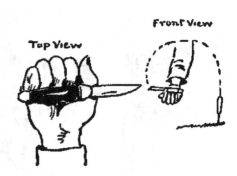

Figs. 282, 283
First and Second Feat

by Dan Beard

Second: The next motion is the same as the first just described, but is performed with the left hand.

Third: Take the point of the blade between the first and second fingers of the right hand, and flip it with a jerk so that the knife turns once around in the air and strikes the point into the ground (Fig. 284).

Fourth: Do the same with the left hand.

Fifth: Hold the knife as in the third and fourth positions, and bring the arm across the chest so that the knife-handle touches the left ear. Take hold of the right ear with the left hand and flip the knife so that it turns once or twice in the air and strikes on its point in the earth (Fig. 285).

Sixth: Do the same with the left hand.

Seventh: Still holding the knife in the same manner, bring the handle up to the nose and fillip it over through the air, so that it will stick in the ground (Fig. 286).

Eighth: Do the same with the handle at the right eye.

Ninth: Repeat, with the handle at the left eye.

Tenth: Place the point of the blade on top of the head. Hold it in place with the forefinger, and with downward push send it whirling down to the earth, where it must stick with the point of blade in the earth (Fig. 287).

Fig. 284
Third Feat

Fig. 285
Fifth Feat

Fig. 286
Seventh Feat

Eleventh to Fifteenth: Hold the left hand with the fingers pointing up, and, beginning with the thumb, place the point of the knife on each finger as described above, and the fore-finger of the forefinger of the right hand on the end of the knife handle. By a downward motion, throw the knife revolving through the air, so that it will alight with the point of the blade in the sod (Fig. 288).

Sixteenth to Twentieth: Repeat, withthe right hand up the left hand on the knife-handle.

Twenty-first, Twenty-second: the same from each knee.

Twenty-third: Hold the point of the blade between the first and second fingers and, placing the band on the forehead, flip the knife back over the head, so that it will stick in the ground behind the player ready for the next motion (Fig. 289; dotted lines show flight of knife).

Twenty-fourth: After twenty-three the knife is left in the ground. Then with the palm of the hand strike the knife handle a smart blow that will send it revolving over the ground for a yard, more or less, and cause it to stick in the ground where it stops. This is called "plowing the field " (Fig. 290; dotted lines show flight of knife).

Fig. 287
Tenth Feat

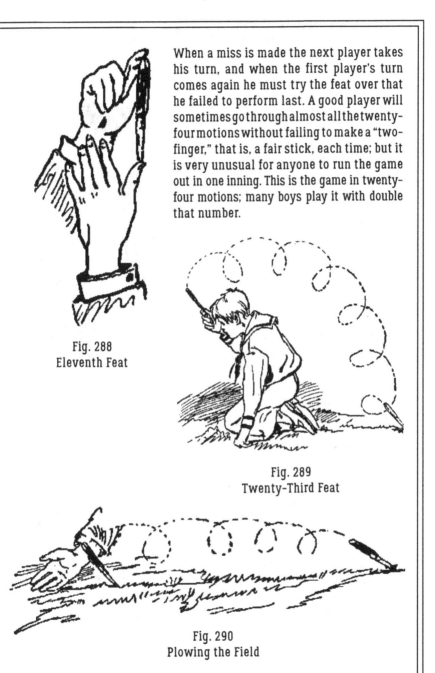

When a miss is made the next player takes his turn, and when the first player's turn comes again he must try the feat over that he failed to perform last. A good player will sometimes go through almost all the twenty-four motions without failing to make a "two-finger," that is, a fair stick, each time; but it is very unusual for anyone to run the game out in one inning. This is the game in twenty-four motions; many boys play it with double that number.

Fig. 288
Eleventh Feat

Fig. 289
Twenty-Third Feat

Fig. 290
Plowing the Field

175

How to Shoot Marbles

Cunny Thumb or Scrumpy Knuckled?

If Little Lord Fauntleroy played marbles, any boy could tell you how he would shoot. He would bold his hand vertically, place his taw or shooter against his thumbnail and his first finger. He would shoot "cunny thumb style," or "scrumpy knuckled." The thumb would flip out weakly (Fig. 5), and the marble would roll on its way.

Tom Sawyer would lay the back of his fist on the ground or on his mole-skin "knuckle dabster," hold his taw between the first and second joints of the second finger and the first joint of the thumb, the three smaller fingers closed and the first finger partially open (Fig. 6). From this animated ballista the marble would shoot through the air for four or five feet, alighting on one of the ducks in the middle of the ring, sending it flying outside, while the taw would spin in the spot vacated by the duck. Tom or Huck Finn would display as much skill with his taw as an expert billiard player would with the ivory balls.

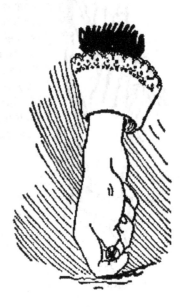

Fig. 5.
"Cunny Thumb"

Fig. 6
As Tom Would Shoot

by Dan Beard

A Southern Way

Down in Dixie I have frequently seen grown men, white and black, playing marbles, and one or two of the expert players held their taw on their second finger, holding the second finger back with their thumb; then suddenly removing the thumb and straightening out the finger, they sent the marble, like a bullet, straight to the mark. This manner of shooting must require much practice, and I doubt if it is more accurate than the one just described as Tom's method. Some boys, skilful in the game, squeeze the marble they shoot with between the thumb ad the forefinger, wetting it with their mouth to make it slip quickly.

Fig. 7
Western Reserve and New York.

Fig. 8
Another and Better Style.

The Arabian Way of Shooting

Arabs have a curious manner of shooting. They place their taw in the hollow between the middle and the forefinger of the left hand, the hand being flat on the ground with the fingers closed. The forefinger of the right hand is then pressed firmly on the end joint of the middle finger, which pushes the middle finger suddenly aside, and the forefinger slips out with sufficient force to propel the shooter very accurately.

There are innumerable games of marbles in vogue in different sections of the country. I have watched the boys play in every State east of the Mississippi River, and between the Gulf of Mexico and the Great Northern Lakes, and will describe the most popular games.

Building a Campfire

"**L**afe, I can't make a fire; we have no paper and the wood's all wet."

Lafe is a Pike County backwoodsman. He only smiled; then shouldering his axe he walked over to a moss-covered log that lay on the ground as soggy and wet as a sponge in the water. With a few blows from the butt end of his axe he knocked out of the rotten wood the remnants of what were once the noble limbs of a giant pine tree. These remnants were now nothing more than spike-shaped clubs, the largest not over two feet long.

Fig. 312
The Fire Won't Burn

"Here's what we use in the woods for paper," said Lafe. Upon examination, we discovered that the spike-shaped clubs were almost as heavy as lead, but it was not water that gave them the weight; it was the sap of the tree, the pitch, that colored them a rich red and made them hard and impervious to rain. Lafe pulled out his one-bladed jackknife and began to whittle the pine stick, but he allowed no shavings to become detached (Fig. 313).

When he had three cut in the manner shown in the accompanying drawing (Fig. 314), he set them up on the ground, with the small ends down and the big ends resting against each other, placed as the sticks are that form the frame of an Indian wigwam. He touched a lighted match to the shavings, and immediately a flame burst forth with a black smoke. Selecting some sticks he had previously split in

Fig. 313
A Fat" Pine Knot

by Dan Beard

halves, he piled them around the blazing pine-knots in a conical wigwam fashion, and soon we had a fire that was hot enough to ignite the wet, unsplit wood we gathered.

Building a Fire Without Matches

After the coffee was boiled and the fish fried and the Boy's clothes partially dried, they made baste to ply Lafe with questions.

"How would you build a fire, if your matches were wet, or if you had none?" asked Tom.

"I generally calculate to keep my matches dry and always keep some about me," answered the woodsman but in case, as you say, I had none, I'd put a light charge of powder in my gun and a loose wad of

Fig. 314
Starting the Fire

cotton rag and shoot in the air, and then double the red-hot ashes of the rag up and blow on it until it flamed up.

"Or, if I that I am running out of matches, I take piece of cotton and dry it at the fire, heating it until it is almost charred; then I dampen the rag and rub gun-powder into its fibers as hard as I can until I can rub no more powder in. After that I dry the rag thoroughly again and put it in a bottle, tin box, or horn, cork it up tight and keep it until I need it. With the back of my knife-blade for a steel and a piece of flint, I strike a spark that sets the rag a-burning and fold the glowing rag tip, cover it with shavings, twisted straw or punk, and blow it into a flame."

Things Worth Remembering

"Tamarack is a very good wood, If you can get it dry, But to make a fire of green tamarack, I'll be a fool to try."

An Indian builds a small campfire and hugs it, a white man makes a roaring big fire and stands away from it.

In selecting a camping-place never forget that the presence of good firewood in abundance is a matter of grave importance. A standing dead cedar will furnish the best of kindling wood. Green, soft woods, spruce, and white birch, burn badly and are difficult to ignite.

To build a fire that will burn all night, select a couple of good heavy sticks for andirons, and a quantity of green hardwood, maple, yellow birch, or beech, for fuel. Across the andirons lay all the fuel sticks in the same direction parallel with each other; in this position they will burn slowly and smolder for a long time. A large tree, or, better still, a large rock at the back of your fire will retain and reflect the heat.

Always select a well-drained spot, or a slight elevation for a place to pitch your tent or build your shack; this will prevent an exceedingly disagreeable experience of awakening during a rain storm to find your tent, floor, and blankets soaked with water. The presence of a neighboring spring, or other water-supply for drinking and cooking, of course, must not be overlooked.

Never pitch your tent in a hollow or depression, or you may find yourself in the middle of a pond. The floor, which is often your bed, can be covered with straw, if straw is obtainable; if not, fir-boughs; these lie flatter than spruce. It is best to lay the foundation of good-sized branches, cover them with smaller ones, and over all place a deep layer of fir twigs broken off the length of your hand, and laid shingle-fashion, commencing at the foot of your bed, or the doorway of your shack or tent, each succeeding row of boughs covering the thick ends of the previous row. A properly made bough bed is as comfortable as a mattress, but one in which the ends of the sticks prod your ribs all night is not a couch that tends to make a comfortable right's rest.

Candles, lamps, and lanterns add to the luggage of a camper, and may be dispensed with, yet it often happens that you will need a light at night. If you do, remember that almost any sort of fat or grease will burn. I have made a passable lamp of an old clam-shell filled with melted rancid butter and a twisted rag for a wick resting in the butter, and I have seen most dainty little candies molded in willow bark of tallow from the deer, with a wick of the inside bark of a cedar-tree. But such things are only made by guides for ladies, or as souvenirs to take home. A torch will answer all needs of camp life.

The Poncho

One of the best piec-es of survival gear ever invented is the windproof and water-proof poncho. Compact and multi-functional, this simple, protective hooded garment can be used in a variety of ways and can even help save your life. It can be used as a shelter, ground bar-rier, or a sleeping bag cover. Reinforced holes called "grommets" on a poncho allow for it to be tied to a tree using

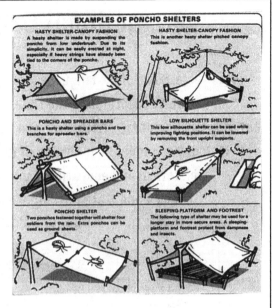

EXAMPLES OF PONCHO SHELTERS

HASTY SHELTER-CANOPY FASHION
A hasty shelter is made by suspending the poncho from low underbrush. Due to its simplicity, it can be easily erected at night, especially if heavy strings have already been tied to the corners of the poncho.

HASTY SHELTER-CANOPY FASHION
This is another hasty shelter pitched canopy fashion.

PONCHO AND SPREADER BARS
This is a hasty shelter using a poncho and two branches for spreader bars.

LOW SILHOUETTE SHELTER
This low silhouette shelter can be used while improving fighting positions. It can be lowered by removing the front upright supports.

PONCHO SHELTER
Two ponchos fastened together will shelter four soldiers from the rain. Extra ponchos can be used as ground sheets.

SLEEPING-PLATFORM AND FOOTREST
The following type of shelter may be used for a longer stay in more secure areas. A sleeping-platform and footrest protect from dampness and insects.

paracord so that it can be used as a sun shade, privacy screen or to block the wind. Without a drinkable water source nearby, a poncho can be used to create a basin to catch rain. It can be used as a makeshift tent or outside of a regular tent to keep gear of firewood dry and can also be used as a way to carry extra gear or collected items such as kindling back to camp.

Depending on the specific style (commonly known as standard, military or backpacking), the poncho can be large enough to accommodate a backpack underneath and allows easy access to gear and a protective firearm. Made of vinyl, polyester, or some other waterproof material, it is usually long enough to sit on, keeping the wearer off of wet ground.

Unlike typical rain gear, the poncho provides for side ventilation that helps to prevent the collection of precipitation. Snaps allow for it to be sealed to keep heat from escaping. By holding a candle lantern between the wearer's knees, the poncho can help seal in heat.

While a good survivalist would never be caught without this "wearable shelter," in an emergency situation, a poncho can be constructed from a waterproof bed sheet and some cord or duct tape.

The 1917 Outdoor School Promotional Catalog

Please note: Some of the language used in this catalog was common and acceptable at the time of its publication, but may be considered "offensive" and "politically incorrect" by today's standards. Inclusion of this catalog is for historical and educational purposes only. Pages 4 and 5 are missing from images.

THE CHIEF

The Dan Beard Outdoor School For Boys

LAKE TEEDYUSKUNG
Pike County, Penn.

Winter Address
EIGHTY-SEVEN BOWNE AVE.
FLUSHING, N. Y.

Summer Address
MASTHOPE, PIKE COUNTY
PENNSYLVANIA

THE DAN BEARD
OUTDOOR SCHOOL FOR BOYS
(INCORPORATED)

DANIEL CARTER BEARD. There is no man identified with the big outdoors and boys' work, more widely known to the parents and more loved by the boys of America, than Dan Beard.

Editor, Author, Artist, Educator and Sportsman, many years member of Board of Education; Past President Campfire Club of America; first honorary member Camp Directors' Association; Past President Society of Illustrators; holder of the gold medal for eminent service, "in recognition of his life's work for the Boys of America"; Founder of the Sons of Daniel Boone and the Boy Pioneers; Life scout; Star scout; Eagle scout; National Scout Commissioner, and Chairman of the National Court of Honor of the Boy Scouts of America. He is, by all who know him, acclaimed as peculiarly fitted for the office of Chief of the unique and delightful school he has founded.

For five years Mr. Beard made a careful and exhaustive study of the outdoor school for boys by conducting one himself. His success proved that his methods are sound, sane and safe.

A year ago last summer he started the Dan Beard Outdoor School, using for the purpose his hunting and fishing lodge on the shores of beautiful Lake Teedyuskung, in the mountains of Pike County, Pennsylvania. The 1917 session of the school will open on June 30th and close August 30th.

183

8 THE DAN BEARD OUTDOOR SCHOOL FOR BOYS

TOTEM BEARERS

184

PURPOSE OF ADVISORY BOARD

OUR ADVISORY BOARD is not a mere list of names. Every man on it is interested in the success of this novel school. Every man on it has expressed his willingness to help by advice, based on his own activities, and many of them have already done so.

The purpose of this is to get practicable view points, in place of theoretical ones. Most schools have heretofore laid special stress on classical studies because the curriculum of the school was arranged almost entirely by teachers and they only saw the needs of their scholars from the standpoint of teachers, and without realizing it, sought to prepare all students to fill places on the faculty as academic instructors, but

THE BOYS OF TO-DAY ARE THE MEN OF TO-MORROW!

The terrible and almost unbelievable consequences of improper education as exemplified by the European war WARNS AMERICA THAT SHE MUST LOOK TO HER BOYS! We claim that the people of the world and of the United States in particular are individually responsible for the careers of the boys and cannot shirk that responsibility. We also claim that the destiny of this country and the world is entirely dependent upon the boys.

Practical knowledge must be added to classical studies in order to properly prepare American boys for life, and as nobody knows more about the requirements of any particular work than the man who is doing it, we have secured for the Advisory Board a group of representative men, occupying positions of prominence in all lines of work.

THE TENTS are pitched in the forests of the Pohopoko Mountains, which are an extension of a wing of the Allegheny range. The camp is on the west shore of an ancient glacier lake, locally known as Big Tink. Elevated 1500 feet above the sea, the west and northwest winds sweep over an unbroken wilderness and the bosom of the lake, bringing with them plenty of ozone, delicately flavored with the perfume peculiar to the breath of the forest. The spring waters and wells are uncontaminated by the presence of dwellings, out-houses or barns. There is nothing to pollute the waters. Last year the school sunk a new well in the woods, which will be used this season.

AWARDING A TOTEM HONOR

A PIKE COUNTY
BULLET POUCH
AND POWDER
HORN

185

10   THE DAN BEARD OUTDOOR SCHOOL FOR BOYS

NATURE AND ROMANCE

ARTHUR BRISBANE has said that childhood is "beautiful and valuable to humanity, because it is the period of strongest imagination."

It is imagination which is the foundation of poetry and art. Imagination is the foundation of all constructive work. The Dan Beard Outdoor School encourages romanticism, because Mr. Beard and his advisers believe that nothing is of greater aid to a boy's mental development than a healthy imagination. This quality of the pupil's mind is fed by stories of adventures of the early pioneers, stories of the forest, of flowers, and animals. The application of the boy's mind to the life surrounding him, is the touch necessary to instil life into dry facts, and make them vital and interesting.

THE CAMP IN THE FOREST

Over one hundrd and forty-seven birds of different species visit or live around the camp, forty-five varieties of trees grow there. A hundred and sixteen varieties of wild flowers and about thirty different mammals have been identified near camp.

12   THE DAN BEARD OUTDOOR SCHOOL FOR BOYS

SPLENDID BATHING FACILITIES ON THE LAKE

OUR SWIMMING PIER extends from the shore to deep water and is safeguarded during swimming hours by three life-savers on the pier and one in a boat.

We believe that accidents to swimmers are almost without exception due to a lack of proper surveillance and care.

The Woodcraft Camps of Daniel Carter Beard

LIFE IN THE OPEN

A PLANT HIKE ON FLOATING LAND

SUCH MEN as Professor Thomas D. Wood, of Columbia University, Rear-Admiral Bradley A. Fiske, U. S. N., and other prominent men, have been quoted as hinting that American is growing "less like a big HE-man than a perfect lady," in other words, that the young men of our nation are what the boys call "sissys." That a few have been softened by luxury may be true.

It is because of an element of truth in these statements that the Dan Beard Outdoor School was founded. This school is essentially red-blooded and masculine. As far as conditions permit, the boys live in the open day and night! Everything possible is done to encourage a love of normal outdoor life.

SCOUT WORK AND METHODS OF STUDY

Classes are held out of doors, and the roof of the study room is the big blue sky. The scout manual of the Boy Scouts of America is used as a text book. The boys sleep in tents which, except during storms, are kept open on all four sides, night and day. The tents are screened to keep out flies and insects. They were especially designed for the Dan Beard Outdoor School and are unusually strong and weather-proof. Their wooden floors are raised well above the ground. The tents are roomy and but two boys are quartered in each tent.

SWIMMING

THERE is no exercise known, which develops a boy's physique, instils self-confidence, gives grace to action and poise, and at the same time brings such joy to a boy's heart as swimming, consequently every pupil of the Dan Beard School will be required to learn how to swim. In order to become a Cub a boy must swim at least fifty feet. Before he can become a Brown Bear, he must be able to dive correctly, recover articles from the bottom and swim at least two hundred yards. Before he can be a Grizzly he must demonstrate the rescue of drowning. All sports and pursuits are conducted under the supervision and guidance of expert directors.

14 THE DAN BEARD OUTDOOR SCHOOL FOR BOYS

TRAMPS AND EXCURSIONS

"**A** THRILL is the main spring of our life, all of us must have it." We supply thrills by over-night excursions in the wilderness, hunts for Indian relics in the caves, hunts for burls on the trees, from which to carve noggins, seach for botanical specimens, search for birds, trees, fish and insects. Then comes the night. With the night comes the thrills! The barred owl shouts in the distance, the timid deer is heard bounding away from the scent of man, or the campers listen to the light footfall of the fox. They also hear the crackling of the camp-fire, and inhale the delicious odor of cooking food, after which they listen to stories and jests—then fall asleep watching the stars winking through the interlacing branches. This gives the boys an experience which they will never forget.

OVER-NIGHT HIKES BY LAND AND WATER

16 THE DAN BEARD OUTDOOR SCHOOL FOR BOYS

THE FACULTY OF THE OUTDOOR SCHOOL

The most successful Americans have been those who have learned the nice adjustments between mental and physical development and who have neglected neither.
Teach a boy to use his physical powers correctly and as a rule he is mentally alert and vigorous.
Such education gives co-ordination of mind and muscle, quick perception, keen sight and acute hearing.

188

The Woodcraft Camps of Daniel Carter Beard

PREPAREDNESS

OUR BOYS, to be helpful in these troublesome times, must be able in an emergency to properly cook food for themselves and others, to bake a bannock, make dough-god, throw a flap-jack so that it will turn in the air and alight in the frying pan, cook meat or fowl with but a green twig for a skewer, properly catch, clean and cook fish or small mammals.

MR. EDMUND
SEYMOUR,
TREASURER OF
THE SCHOOL

EACH BOY LEARNS TO PREPARE AND COOK
A MEAL IN THE OPEN

ful

have

mental
ment
ected

se
rrectly
ntally

ination
quick
ght

SOME OF THE BEST BOYS WHO EVER ATTENDED SCHOOL.

18   THE DAN BEARD OUTDOOR SCHOOL FOR BOYS

CLASS IN FIRST AID AND FIRST AID TENT

MEDICAL ATTENDANCE

IT IS OUR PLAN, as it was last year, to have a practising physician on the school grounds, who will be in constant attendance throughout the entire term and we also expect to have a practical dentist with us, as we did last year, to examine the boys' teeth and report whenever they need attention.

LOG ROLLING DAY FOR THE TRADING POST

The Woodcraft Camps of Daniel Carter Beard

RELIGIOUS SERVICES IN GOD'S OWN CATHEDRAL

RELIGIOUS INFLUENCES

MEN OF ACTION, men of the open, are never atheists or agnostics, such terms were practically unknown among the early Americans. The faculty are men of action who will exert a religious but undenominational influence. Ministers of various religious sects will be invited to speak to the boys.

HANDICRAFT

THE BOYS build themselves shacks, shanties and shelters for over-night hikes, they make bridges without nails or ropes, they make ditty bags of hides and skins, knife sheathes for their bacon knives and all other appliances and trinkets of the woods which delight the heart of a boy, and give skill to his fingers and alertness to his mind.

HANDICRAFT, THINGS THE BOYS MAKE
1—Buckskin ditty bag; 2—Whang leather ditty bag; 3—Oil tanned buckskin bag; 4—Hatchet scabbard; 5—Camp axe scabbard; 6—Camp knife scabbard; 7—Rawhide knife scabbard; 8—Fire board for fire making outfit; 9, 10, 11, 12—Noggins or drinking cups; 13—Thimble for fire spindle; 14—Ash holder for hearth or fire board; 15, 16—Flasks for toilet; 17—Needle case; 18, 19—Fire bows.

CAMP FORMATION

HONOR MEN

ON ENTERING THE SCHOOL, the boy is assigned to a group known as a "stockade." Each group is composed of eight boys and a leader, with a totem pole of its own. On the top of the pole is the heraldic totem animal.

THE DAN BEARD HONOR SYSTEM

In all competitive work, such as inspection of tents, inspection of person (which includes not only dress, condition of hands and finger-nails, but also the condition of the teeth), and in competitive games the winning stockade is rewarded by a red white and blue streamer with a brass sleigh-bell at one end, which is fastened to the totem pole. The poorest stockade receives a "boob" or "chump" mark —a ribbon of yellow which is fastened to the totem pole. At the end of the term, the totem staffs at formation present a striking appearance. Back of the idea is the fostering of a healthy spirit or rivalry and esprit-de-corps.

For every deed of conspicuous merit a pupil is decorated by a red white and blue ribbon, known as a "nick," which is worn above the heart.

STUDIES

THE STUDY ROOM IS
ALL OUTDOORS

IF DESIRED, boys may receive without extra charge careful coaching in the following subjects: Arithmetic, Elementary Algebra, English Grammar, English Composition, Public Speaking, Reading, Writing, Mental Arithmetic and Spelling. Victor Aures of the Albright Art School, of Buffalo will teach Drawing—(one and one-half hour required for preparation and recitation.

This affords an opportunity to each boy to strengthen himself in any study in which he may not be up to the mark, or to do the extra work necessary if he desires to skip a grade.

The Woodcraft Camps of Daniel Carter Beard

HONOR MARKS

TEN NICKS make a notch, which is an honor mark worn on the left sleeve of the uniform. Besides these merit notches, there are special notches for expertness in forestry, fire-building, pioneering, plant-knowledge, bird-knowledge, etc. Should a boy do anything mean or unmanly, or commit a stupid or thoughtless blunder he must wear the chump mark (a yellow ribbon) on his right breast for at least one week. At the end of the week, he may remove the chump mark by the surrender of two "nicks."

THE BUCKSKIN BOYS

THOSE BOYS who prove themselves trustworthy and consistently honorable form a group called the Buckskin Boys. The Buckskin Boys are entitled to wear the coveted Buckskin Badge, a fringed ornament emblazoned with a pioneer powder horn. This badge is more highly prized among the boys than any decoration they can win, for its wearer is the first to be called for any duty requiring absolute dependability and efficiency. The Buckskin Boys are known to be thoroughly reliable and their word can be trusted under the most trying circumstances.

THE MUCH COVETED
BUCKSKIN BADGE

THE MESS

THE MESS-HALL is an open pavilion, screened on all sides to keep out flies and insects. It is thirty by sixty feet, and the tables are furnished with linen, china and silver. The waiters are uniformed in white duck and the meals have been pronounced equal to those served at first-class country hotels.

It is planned to give the boys well balanced rations of simple and wholesome food. The hearty appetites aroused by vigorous exercise in the open, offers a splendid opportunity to teach the boys to crave and enjoy proper and nutritious food.

MESS HALL   STEWARD AND STAFF

TABLE MANNERS

IN order that the pupils may not revert to young savages, the tables are set practically as they would be at home. The stockade leader and one of the instructors sit at each table. It is their duty not only to direct the conversation, but also to see that the boys sit properly, use their knife and fork in the proper manner and eat properly. The boys march in to mess, stand at attention during a silent grace, until the order "Seats!" is given. When seated they remain at attention with arms folded until the command "Rest!" is heard, then the meal begins. Everything is conducted in a proper and gentlemanly manner.

26   THE DAN BEARD OUTDOOR SCHOOL FOR BOYS

COUNCIL FIRE

EVERY NIGHT there is a camp fire, around which the boys assemble to throw their tomahawks and listen to stories of Daniel Boone, Simon Kenton and George Washington, and all the big, splendid, moral men of the early days.

On Saturday nights the council fire blazes, distinguished visitors address the boys, buckskin men are accepted and honors distributed. These council fires are strikingly picturesque.

28   THE DAN BEARD OUTDOOR SCHOOL FOR BOYS

EQUIPMENT AND TERMS

THESE BOYS WILL NOT BE WEIGHED IN
THE BALANCE AND FOUND WANTING

THE COMFORT and success of camp life depend very largely upon equipment. The equipment of this camp is the result of many years of experiment to determine just what is essential for a boy to have in order to make camp life healthful, comfortable and of the greatest benefit.

The cost of the entire term is $200.00, payable on entrance. This covers board and tuition.

We regret to announce that war prices make it impossible for the school to supply the boys with their personal equipment, as was done during the summer of 1916.

The Woodcraft Camps of Daniel Carter Beard

INSISTENCE ON AMERICAN IDEALS

IN SUCH TRYING TIMES as these, the management of the Dan Beard School feels that it can best serve parents, pupils and the nation at large by recalling the glorious deeds of the pioneers to their youthful descendants and firing their hearts and minds, in the crucial formative period, with the inspiration that gave birth to this Republic.

AMERICAN HONOR MARKS

THE TRADING POST

THERE will be a Post Office and Trading Post where the students may buy postal cards, postage stamps, toilet articles, etc.

Credit will be given at the Trading Post only when an account has been authorized by the parents. All requisitions for articles which are to be charged must be approved by an officer of the school before they will be honored. The Trading Post is for the convenience of the pupils and the faculty.

HOW TO GET THERE

THE NEAREST STATIONS to the Dan Beard School are Masthope, Pennsylvania, and Rowlands, Pennsylvania. Masthope is on the main line of the Erie Railroad, 117 miles from New York City; Rowlands is 116 miles from New York City. There are trains from New York on the Erie Railroad direct to these two points. From Cincinnati, Cleveland, Chicago, Buffalo and points west there are trains to Masthope on the Erie Railroad. Rowlands may be reached from points southwest by way of Scranton. Time tables will be sent to applicants.

AUTOMOBILE ROUTE

By automobile the camp is 133 miles from New York, 130th Street. Take Fort Lee ferry, turn to the right and follow the river about a mile, then to the left up a steep hill, thence to Hackensack Court House, Hohokus, Suffern, Tuxedo, Monroe, East Chester, Goshen, Slate Hill, Port Jervis, Milford.

At Milford be very careful to turn to the left at Farmers' Hotel, then follow guide posts along State road to Hawley. When you reach Hawley take the road to Forest Lake Club. This road passes through our camp.

ANOTHER ROUTE

A shorter trip is via Dyckman Street ferry, Englewood, Paterson, Pompton, Newfoundland, Franklin Furnace, Branchville, Dingmans and Milford, thence as above described.

CAUTION: There are two roads to Hawley and Honesdale. Take the road to the left at Farmers' Hotel for it is the better road.

THE MEN RESPONSIBLE FOR THE CALL OF THE
WILD AND THE BOYS WHO ANSWERED THE CALL

The Woodcraft Camps of Daniel Carter Beard

DAN BEARD OUTDOOR SCHOOL APPLICATION

The 1917 Course Will Begin June 30th and End August 30th

As only a limited number of boys can be received this season, an early application is desirable. This application is, of course, merely an expression of intention and in no way binding should anything serious occur to prevent the attendance of the applicant.

I desire to enter my son in the DAN BEARD OUTDOOR SCHOOL, Summer Course, beginning June 30th and ending August 30th, 1917.

City...State...

Name in Full...

Residence Address ....

Business Address of Father..

Age..Height............................... Weight.....................

School last Attended...

Signature...

The right is reserved to reject the application of any boy whom the school authorities believe to be an undesirable addition to the camp. It is essential to impress upon parent or guardian signing this application that it is understood that the boy for whom the application is made has no characteristic which will make him an undesirable companion for other boys.

Only boys who can remain the full period of the course will be admitted. In case of suspension or dismissal or in case of voluntary withdrawal, no part of the cost of board, tuition or equipment will be refunded. In case of sickness, when a boy is detained from school for more than one week, twelve dollars per week will be refunded.

THE CALL OF THE WILD

BACK OF THIS SCHOOL and giving it moral and substantial support is a typical group of wilderness men, representatives to-day of the sturdy, buckskin clad pioneers of yesterday. These men are prominent in the business and professional world, and many of them are internationally known in the fields of exploration, science and literature. They are big, red-blooded men, intensely human, and with real old-fashioned hearts under their vests, the sort of characters which win every boy's admiration and affection. It is because of a life-long association with such men that the Chief was inspired to launch and conduct this outdoor school. The top photograph shows a group of these men taken at Pike on a mid-winter hike over the mountains. Standing from right to left are Edmund Seymour, our Treasurer; Julius H. Seymour, our Legal Adviser; George L. Hubbell, Vice-President of the Campfire Club; The Chief and Elmore Gregor. Seated in front are Charles Tatham and Ottomar H. Van Norden, directors of the Dan Beard Company, and devotees of out-door life.

197

THE FIRST WOODCRAFTERS

CULVER SUMMER SCHOOL OF WOODCRAFT, 1912

Thirty-six boys were in attendance for the first eight-week session of the Woodcraft Camp.

ALABAMA
Lewis, R. M.

COLORADO
Pressnal, D. D.

ILLINOIS
Bolton, J. C.
Britton, W. A.
Kindig, J.K.

INDIANA
Blair, J. P.
Bilow, P. E.
Butman, C. V.
(One Unidentified)

KANSAS
Jackson, S. L., Jr.

KENTUCKY
Reeves, C. G.
Williams, S.

LOUISIANA
Dodge, E. H.
Faucett, J. E.
Googins, D. S.

MISSOURI
Culver, W. L.
Long, P.

OHIO
Boardman, J. K.
Campbell, R. C.
Clark, C. S.
Crapo, F. M.
Engle, A. J.
Feldmann, C. X.
Logan, W. M.
Miller, J. G.
Moore, P. M.
Orwig, A. R.
Ulmer, J. J.

PENNSYLVANIA
Arnstine, J. M.
Gelders, J. S.
Morse, R. N., Jr.

TEXAS
Googins, J. C.
Hutchings, S., Jr.
Morgan, H. I.
Richards, L. H.

LIST OF APPLICATIONS* FOR THE DAN BEARD OUTDOOR SCHOOL FOR BOYS, 1916 AND 1917.
*Library of Congress

1916

1. Richards, S. A.
2. Edwards, David
3. Macklin, Maxwell
4. Atwater, Edward
5. Thompson, W.
6. Owens, Donnie (reneged)
7. Rich, Edwards
8. Brewington, Marion V.
9. Barnes, J. Edward
10. Geer, D. Reed
11. Miller, Wm. Hurxthal
12. Vilas, Royal Lee
13. Fargo, Walter G.
14. Smith, Carlile B.
15. Griffith, Dick
16. Mikell, Waring
17. Cranage, Thomas
18. Kurtz, Charles T.
19. Kurtz, Robert M.
20. Williams, Byard
21. Williams, Clarke
22. LeRoy, Newbold
23. Tupper, Thomas
24. Emeny, Brooks
25. Austin, Albert M.
26. Edwards, William S.
27. Gaines, John M.
28. Gaines, Pierce W.
29. Ross, John C.
30. Kirkpatrick, Jas. T.
31. Hughes, Howard R.
32. Clark, Charles W.
33. Moise, B. C.
34. Fink, Donald
35. Zinser, August, 3rd
36. Holcombe, Alexander, Jr.
37. Schalck, Lyman G.
38. Fulghum, Bennie
39. Hughes, Rush
40. Ahlborn, Hewey D.
41. Lachlan, Bruce S. (reneged)
42. Farr, Jack
43. Jekyll, Arthur

1917

1. Geissler, Allen Moore
2. Geissler, Duval Kenneth
3. LeRoy, Newbold (2nd year)
4. Mikell, Waring (2nd year)
5. Jones, Nat, M.
6. Edwards, Wm. Seymour (2nd year)
7. Griffith, Dick (2nd year) (reneged)
8. Potter, Eastman
9. Von Storch, Connie
10. Hubbard, William S.
11. McClintoe, Walter L.
12. Fulghum, Bennie (2nd year)
13. Edwards, David (2nd year)
14. Atwater, David T.
15. Jekyll, Arthur (2nd year)
16. Martin, Paul
17. Salmon, John
18. Churchman, Morgan
19. Kitson, Jackson
20. Kitson, James
21. Buhl, Paul
22. Payer, Franklin
23. Bixby, Allen
24. Wallace, Frederick
25. Snyder, Jack
26. Fuller, Andrew (deceased)
27. Lockwood, Henry
28. Geer, Reed (2nd year)
29. Barnes, Homer
30. Myers, Richmond
31. Austin, Albert (2nd year)
32. Stineman, Cameron
33. Howe, Daniel
34. Crowther, David
35. Hamilton, Horace
36. Hastings, Charles
37. Warren, Tarbet
38. Mccutcheon, James
39. Kempner, Isaac
40. Churchman, Richard
41. Euston, Alexander
42. Euston, Elmer
43. Dotson, Henry
44. Emeny, Brooks (2nd year)
45. Emeny, Brooke
46. Hodgson, Kaspar (1 month)
47. Kerans, Jack
48. Klots, George (1 month)
49. Milton, Paul
50. Schalck, Lyman (2nd year)
51. Shepperd, Gwynn Ellis
52. Wetherill, John
53. HUGHES, HOWARD (2nd year)
54. Sharp, Dudley
55. Beard, Bartlett
56. Blum, Leon Marx
57. McDonald, Arthur (reneged)
58. Ellsworth, Van Renseller (reneged)

3 reneges
11 second year boys

#2-A Beaconsfield Apts.
Houston, Tex.
Dec. 29, 1916.

Dear Chief,

I was glad to get your letter, and I hope that I can come to your camp next year, and bring my friend Dudley Sharp. I have joined the Y. M. C. A. and like it very much. Enclosed please find my Buckskin Badge. I have returned it on account of eating some candy.

With love from.
Howard.

P. S. I hope that you and Mrs. Beard and Bartlett and Barbara have a Happy New Year.

HOWARD HUGHES RETURNS BUCKSKIN BADGE TO DAN BEARD
In this letter, Howard Hughes felt compelled to confess
to Chief Beard about having eaten some candy.

Courtesy of the Library of Congress Manuscript Collection.

201

THE BUCKSKIN MEN

This is a band of SPARTANS, a chosen lot of boys of character and will-power. Each boy when elected wears a badge of buckskin on which is branded the powder horn of Daniel Boone. To win this award, a boy must be absolutely truthful, thoroughly reliable and have sufficient control of his own appetite to govern it even when subjected to severe temptation. "THE BUCKSKIN MEN" is a society for building character, as one would build muscle, by exercising. The badge was the most highly prized one in the school.

A famous Buckskin Man initiates the new Buckskin Men usually during an overnight campfire ceremony with an ancient Indian initiation, which was exceedingly picturesque but, of course secret. The council fire ceremony was solemn and impressive, but not rough. Each boy or man swore to the Buckskin Law:

1. A Buckskin Man is true.
2. A Buckskin Man is faithful.
3. A Buckskin Man makes good.
4. A Buckskin Man is not greedy of gain or glory.
5. A Buckskin Man will stand alone for the right.
6. A Buckskin Man denies himself for the good of others.
7. A Buckskin Man values his honor more than his life.
8. A Buckskin man never deserts his comrade.

BUCKSKIN PLEDGE/LAW:
A Buckskin man is first and above all a loyal and enthusiastic American.
A Buckskin Man obeys the Scout Law.
A Buckskin Man believes that usefulness is the highest quality of morality.
A Buckskin Man possesses all the chivalry of a cavalier, all the friendliness of a Quaker, all the bravery, loyalty, hospitality, and joyousness of a Buckskin Scout of the early frontier; hence, a Buckskin Man's honor means more to him than his property or even his fife.

BUCKSKIN OATH/PROMISE
Standing here in the presence of Almighty God and the people here assembled, I avow and affirm that, because I want to be a Buckskin Man, I of my own free will and choice, give my solemn pledge and promise to live according to the Buckskin Law.

Books by Daniel Carter Beard

To learn more about the woodcrafts and skills that were taught at Dan Beard's camps, you can research the following books:

- *The American Boy's Handy Book** (1882) (1903)
- *The American Boy's Book of Sport* (1890)
- *The Outdoor Handy Book** (1896)
- *The Jack of All Trades: New Ideas for American Boys** (1900)
- *The Field and Forest Handy Book: New Ideas for Out of Doors** (1906)
- *Handicraft for Outdoor Boys* (1906)
- *Animal Book and Campfire Stories* (1907)
- *The Boy Pioneers: Sons of Daniel Boone* (1909)
- *Boat Building, and Boating** (1912)
- *Shelters, shacks, and Shanties** (1920) (2012)
- *The American Boy's Book of Bugs, Butterflies and Beetles* (1915)
- *The American Boy's Book of Signs, Signals and Symbols* (1918)
- *The Book of Camp-Lore and Woodcraft** (1920)
- *The American Boy's Book of Wild Animals* (1921)
- *The Black Wolf-Pack* (1922)
- *American Boy's Book of Birds and Brownies of the Woods* (1923)
- *Do It Yourself Bushcraft* (1925)
- *Wisdom of the Woods* (1926)
- *Buckskin Book For Buckskin Men and Boys* (1929)
- *Hardly A Man is Now Alive* (1939)

*titles still in print

BIBLIOGRAPHY

ARCHIVAL COLLECTIONS

Bear Mountain Trailside Museum, Bear Mountain, New York

The Daniel Carter Beard Memorial collection was donated by Beard's children, Bartlett and Barbara. They felt it appropriate to have an exhibit near Beard's home at Suffern, New York.

The Beard room, a twenty-six feet long reproduction of a room in "Uncle Dan's" razed home in Suffern, New York, contains the large fireplace and mantel complete with artifacts from his collection of pioneer and Indian lore relics. The drawing board, brushes and paints Beard used to make his famous illustrations for the first editions of such books as Mark Twain's A Connecticut Yankee in King Arthur's Court and Tom Sawyer Abroad have also been placed in the memorial room.

A picture exhibition illustrates the span of Beard's life and career. Diaries, family albums, family heritage, books, uniforms, awards, newspaper articles and notices, lectures, and letter correspondence to and from associates, Presidents, and celebrities are available through the B.T.B. Hyde Memorial Library located at the north end of the museum building.

Culver Academies Historical Archives – Digital Vault

Campus Buildings: A photographic display of Culvers stately campus structures, early to most recent.

Summer Publications: Culver summer schools and the woodcraft camps.

Vedette: Culver Academies student newspaper from 1896 – present.

Woodcraft photos: An assortment of Culver woodcraft camp photos, 1912 – 1990s.

Lackawaxen Township, Pike county, Pennsylvania, Public Records Review

A review of the years 1887 – 1938.

Library of Congress Manuscript collection (LCMC): Daniel Carter Beard Papers

The papers of Daniel Carter Beard were presented to the Library of Congress by his estate on July 17, 1941. A substantial source for this book, the papers total some 72,000 pieces, with the greatest number dated between the years 1915 and 1935. The collection contains correspondence to and from Beard. Drafts of his lectures, letters and memoranda from Boy Scout leaders, Culver Woodcraft School and the Dan Beard Outdoor School. Several boxes hold newspaper articles and notices gathered by Beard's clipping service. The collection has personal testimonials from the Outdoor School. The collection is one of the largest and most neglected in the Library of congress. SPECIAL NOTE: The Beard papers in the Library of Congress Manuscript Collection (LCMC) have been re-processed since my inspection in 1974.

Susan Munson Boyle Collection: 1994.82.18 National Scouting Museum Archives

This collection consists of photographs, writings, correspondence, diaries, annual reports and scrapbooks concerning the Dan Beard Outdoor School compiled, drafted or photographed by Susan Munson Boyle. She was the secretary performing operational, clerical and/or office managerial duties from 1915 – 1925.

PERSONAL AND TELEPHONE INTERVIEWS, LETTER AND E-MAIL CORRESPONDENCE

Aures, Victor – telephone interview, Outdoor School promotion pamphlets used by the author were sent by Mr. Aures, a former counselor and instructor at the Outdoor School.

Baker, Andrew and Crossley, Pare' Vicki – Culver Academies Huffington Public Library. Telephone conversations, Ms. Crossley sent to the author Culver woodcraft newspaper articles from The Culver Citizen (local newspaper) and The Vedette (Culver Military Academy newspaper).

Beard, Barbara – daughter of Daniel Beard, telephone interview and letter correspondence, November and December, 1974.

Beard, Bartlett – son of Daniel Beard, personal interview May 24, 1974 in Santa Fe, New Mexico, and personal correspondence during November and December, 1974.

Carr, William – personal interview, May 28, 1974 in Tucson, Arizona. Mr. Carr, a personal friend of the Beard family helped structure the Beard Room at Bear Mountain Trailside Museum, Bear Mountain, New York.

Dodd, Edward – telephone interview and letter correspondence, creator of the Mark Trail comic strip, and was in charge of the daily Outdoor School camp operation during the 1920's.

Ersbak, Ken – letter correspondence, Forest Lake Club Manager. Club members took a keen interest in the Outdoor School from 1916 -1938 sending a large delegation on Saturday evenings to the weekly Council Fire programs.

Finney, Alice – telephone interview and letter correspondence, visited the Outdoor School with her mother who directed Camp Douglas, a camp for girls located on Lake Teedyuskung.

Gammons, Bradley – Grandson of Albert Trexler, a personal friend of Dan Beard. Assisted the author with personal communications between Trexler and Beard.

Gibbons, Patricia – telephone interview, Ms. Gibbons sent the author a DVD video with pictures of the Outdoor School and information concerning the moving of the Outdoor School Camp Headquarters from Hawley, Pennsylvania to land owned by the Northeastern Pennsylvania Region of the Boy Scouts of America.

Gilbert, Daniel F. – letter correspondence, son of D.C. Gilbert, an instructor of handicraft at the Outdoor School for twelve years.

James, Dorie – telephone interview, 1974 and 1993, father attended the Outdoor School as a teenager.

Kenney, Jeff – telephone interview and e-mail correspondence, Culver Communications Department, assisted author with images and authenticity concerning the Culver Woodcraft Summer Camp for Boys.

Mikel, Warring – letter correspondence, camper at the Outdoor School in 1916 and 1917.

Salomon, Julian H. – personal interview, August 18, 1974 in Suffern, New York. Mr. Salomon was a personal friend of Dan Beard and instructor at the Outdoor School during World War I.

Trexler, Albert – personal interview, June 1994 in Kempton, Penna. Mr. Trexler was a personal friend of the Beard family.

Trone, Peter – telephone interviews November 14 and December 17 of 1974 (Outdoor School camper).

Whitton, Beaumert – letter correspondence, camper and junior leader at the Outdoor School.

Willis, Howie L. – letter correspondence November 24, 1974, camper and instructor at the Culver Woodcraft Summer School, 1918 to 1925.

BOOKS

Beard, Daniel C. The American Boys' Handy Book: What to Do and How to Do It. New York, Scribner's and Sons, 1882. Jack of All Trades. New York, Scribner's and Sons, 1900. Shelters, Shackes, and Shanties, Charles Scribner's and Son, 1914. The Buckskin Book for Buckskin Boys. J. B. Lippencott, 1929. Camp Lore and Woodcraft. Dover Publications, Mineola, New York, 2006 (a reprint from the 1920 edition).

Clemens, Cyril and Sibley, Carroll. Uncle Dan: The Life Story of Dan Beard, New York, Thomas Y. Crowell Co. 1938.

Hartman, Robert. Hartman on History. Culver historian for the Culver Educational Academy, (available on Google).

Hillcourt, William. Baden-Powell: The Two Lives of a Hero. New York, G.P. Putnam's and sons, 1964.

Lackawaxen Township Bicentennial Book: 200 years of growth, 1998.

Phillips, John. Selling America: The Boy Scouts of America in the Progressive Era, 1910 – 1921. Master's thesis, University of Maine, 2001.

Rice, Emmett A., Hutchinson, John J. and Lee, Mabel. A Brief History of Physical Education. New York, the Ronald Press, 1958.

Roeder, Mark A. A History of Culver and The Culver Military Academy. New York, iUniverse press, Inc. 1993 and 2004.

Rowen, Edward L. M.D. To Do My Duty: James E. West and the History of the Boy Scouts of America. Exeter, N.H., Publishing works, 2005.

Willis, Chuck. Boy Scouts of America: A Centennial History, New York, D. K. Publishing, 2009.

Zimmerman, Dick Maj. <u>Culver Academies Woodcraft Camp 75th Anniversary History Book</u>, Culver Academies, 1987. (Maj. Zimmerman longtime woodcraft and Indian lore instructor for over fifty years wrote a history of the woodcraft program emphasizing: The scouting programs – the Indian lore and council fire programs – the bird sanctuary – and the book has a photo-filled history of the woodcraft program).

MAGAZINE ARTICLES

Beard, Daniel C. - <u>Boys' Life Magazine</u>

August 1912 – "Woodcraft Camp – Culver Academy"

October 1912 – "Culver Academy Outdoor School"

January 1913 – "Something About Buckskin Men"

February 1913 – "Boys of today – Men of Tomorrow"

June 1914 – "A Stacker With 'Sacred Medicine'"

October 1914 – "How to Use an Axe"

July 1915 – Dan Beard Tells You How to Make a Noggin"

October 1915 – "My Experiences with the Boys at the Culver Woodcraft Camp"

August 1916 – "Dan Beard Tells You How: Trail Marks"

August 1917 – "Trailing the Way and How to do It"

November 1917 – "How to Build Your Own Rifle Range"

March 1918 – "How to Build a Council Ring and Fire"

June 1918 – "Eagle Scout tells about Dan Beard Outdoor School"

September 1918 – "Woodcraft Stunts"

October 1918 – "Gossiping with Dan Beard: Buckskin Men's Law and Oath"

January 1919 – "Winter Hiking"

May 1920 – "Camping Hints from the Chief Scout"

October 1920 – "Laying Out the Council Grounds"

August 1922 – "Practical tips on Camping"

December 1922 – "The Use of the Tomahawk"

March 1929 – "How to build a Fort Pitt Door"

February 1932 – "Make Your Plans Now for Camping"

February 1937 – "Winter Hiking and Camping"

Gibson, Dana – Boys' Life Magazine, February 1925, "My Friend Dan Beard"

Broome, Bertram – Boys' Life Magazine, March 1926, "The School of Distinction"

Chisholm, Elizabeth – (LCMC), Red Book "Camp tour"

Fisher, George – Boys' Life Magazine, August 1938, "Uncle Dan"

Kahler, William V. – Mark Twain Journal, Winter, 1976 – 77, "Mark Twain: Adult Hero of Daniel Carter Beard"

PERSONAL CORRESPONDENCES

Aures, Victor to William Carr – February 20, 1974 (letter sent to author by Mr. Carr)

Beard, Dan to John Alexander – September 6, 1912 (LCMC)

Beard, Dan to Col. L. R. Gignilliat – December 9, 1914 (LCMC)

Beard, Dan to Howard Hughes, Sr. – July 11, 1916 (LCMC)

Beard, Dan to Howard Hughes, Sr. – August 7, 1916 (LCMC)

Beard, Dan to Allene Hughes – August 28, 1916 (LCMC)

Gignilliat, Col. L.R. to Dan Beard – February 15, March 2 and 12, 1912 October 11, 1915 (LCMC)

Hughes, Allene to Dan Beard – June 14, 1916 (LCMC)

Hughes, Allene to Victor Aures – July 16, 1917 (LCMC)

Hughes, Allene to Dan Beard – July 17, 1916 (LCMC)

Hughes, Allene to Dan Beard – October 14. 1917 (LCMC)

Hughes, Howard Jr. to Dan Beard – December 29, 1916 (LCMC)

Hughes, Howard Sr. to Dan Beard – June 30, 1916 (LCMC)

March, Alvin to James E. West – September 12, 1912 (LCMC)

West James E. to Dan Beard – September 9, 1912 (LCMC)

WEB SITES

Amazon.com/throwing-hatchet-Boy Scouts-lightweight/dp/BOOD12LR18

Boy Scouts of America National Shooting Sports Manual – No. 430-938

Cilawoodsmen.ca/rules/event-rules/axe-throw

Productimages.knife-depot.com/e8/7_541505.jpg

PIKE COUNTY COURT HOUSE

Deed Book 45, page 89, 49, page 216, 60, page 189, 69, page 146 – researched by Ronald M. Bugaj Attorney, Honesdale, Pennsylvania

Printed in the United States
by Baker & Taylor Publisher Services